PRAISE FOR *YOUTH VIOLENCE PREVENTION: THE PATHWAY BACK THROUGH INCLUSION AND CONNECTION*

"A great resource and guide for school and district leaders based on actual, practical, and relevant scenarios and events. A must-read for educators and those who work on ensuring and maintaining student safety in a school setting. The authors are actual practitioners with decades of firsthand knowledge and experience in how to manage, facilitate, and resolve such critical and complex situations and incidents."—Salam A. Noor, PhD, former chief state schools officer for Oregon and currently president and CEO of Education Consultants International, LLC

"This book illuminates both the logistical and programmatical steps in assuring a successful assessment program through a lens of equity, which often goes overlooked in the analysis of behavioral threats on our school campuses. Through student voice, schools can capitalize on what matters most, balancing inclusion and restorative practices in a manner that is fair for all."—Dr. Hank Gutierrez, deputy superintendent, office of the Fresno County Superintendent of Schools, Fresno, California

"*Youth Violence Prevention: The Pathway Back through Inclusion and Connection* builds on the research-based practices developed and implemented by John Van Dreal and his colleagues around student threat assessment. The authors, based on their years of experience in education, have a laser-like focus on disrupting the school-to-prison pipeline by providing a comprehensive road map on how to reengage students through prevention, interventions, and community connections."—Mary Paulson, deputy executive director, Oregon School Boards Association

"As longtime educators, mental health professionals, and violence prevention experts, the Van Dreals and McCarthy provide a proven model of school behavioral threat assessment and management that educators, mental health professionals, and law enforcement professionals identify with. The valuable case studies for prevention of youth violence provide threat assessment teams and school personnel with critical steps in securing information for appropriate collaborative intervention. *Youth Violence Prevention: The Pathway Back through Inclusion and Connection* is essential for anyone working to identify, assess, and prevent youth violence."—Tom Kelley, training and education specialist, Texas School Safety Center

"As a threat assessment professional, I would highly recommend this book to school district threat assessment teams. The authors have crafted a text that provides realistic and complex cases along with insightful and practical questions for further team discussion. A perfect training supplement to *Assessing Student Threats: Implementing the Salem-Keizer System, Second Edition* by John Van Dreal et al."—Joseph E. Holifield, PhD, threat management coordinator, Behavioral Health Assessment and Response Project (B-HARP), San Luis Obispo, California

"What sets these authors apart from so many others is that their work is anchored in decades of *real-life* experience in dealing with student threats and threat assessments in the public school setting. This rare level of experience allows the Salem-Keizer Cascade Model to guide assessors toward a response that is neither overreactive nor underreactive. This book will be an invaluable resource for training school administrators, mental health professionals, and law enforcement personnel in implementing the Salem-Keizer Cascade Model. Many of the students depicted in the book's case studies will immediately be 'recognizable' by any educator with even a few years of student management experience, and walking the reader through the assessment considerations in these specific cases will undoubtedly translate to a better prepared and more effective assessment team member."—Joseph Parks, JD, (retired) executive director of Safety and Security Services, Plano Independent School District; Lieutenant (retired) Plano Police Department, Plano, Texas

"If you are a school administrator or an SRO or have another role in school security, you need this book for your toolbox. The cases presented could happen in any school around the world, and the behavioral-based approach for assessing and intervening in each case is straightforward. When used as intended, the Salem-Keizer Cascade threat assessment system works to avoid bias and is 100% student centered."—Neil Musser, assistant principal and director of safety and security, Ellensburg School District, Ellensburg, Washington

"Success for teachers, students, and families in overcoming trauma or crisis situations within a school community must be steeped in preventive measures. This book is a wonderful resource to build positive intervention strategies to assist any school district in creating that security lens!"—Carlene Yell, MEd, assistant principal, director Federal Programs, Maryetta Public Schools, Stilwell, Oklahoma

"John Van Dreal, Coleen Van Dreal, and Courtenay McCarthy's work is highly respected, and their book is a must-read for anyone in the field of student threat assessment. The case scenarios and the Salem-Keiser Cascade Model prepare school teams for real-life threat assessments. This guide provides a gold-standard process for those working in the field."—Dan Beaudoin, student support coordinator, student threat assessment coordinator, Capital Region ESD 113, Tumwater, Washington

"John Van Dreal and his colleagues' approaches and content are operationally and best-practices based and serve well those in the threat assessment and management arenas. I've had the benefit of working with John in recent years and have found his wisdom and practices superlative. I consider John a leader in his field and have even incorporated his approaches and content into my professional services in the public and private sectors. I've come across multiple models for threat assessment and management in the school arenas, and I have found John's approaches and model to be the clearest and most operationally sound. John brings a wealth of multidimensional information and experience to the table; you don't want to miss out!"—Manny Tau, PsyD, CTM; clinical and forensic psychologist, Certified Threat Manager

"When our district felt there was a potential threat, we were so relieved to have the Salem-Keizer Cascade student threat assessment framework to know when to complete an assessment, whom to involve, and how to evaluate the possible threat. We also learned how to really identify needs for interventions and supports in a way that has helped decrease risk and increase academic success for all students. We have been grateful to know how to approach these situations by following these violence prevention protocols and training tools."—Miriam Campbell, LCSW, Provo City School District, Provo, Utah"The Salem-Keizer Cascade Model provides our six-county region in Western Colorado with a preventative, proactive system grounded in collaboration to keep children safe. Its power is showcased in these case studies. While there is no simple solution to assessing threats, the model embraces the 'grey' of these situations while empowering threat assessment teams with interventions for the student exhibiting threatening behavior that are not necessarily reliant on the courts or the mental health system. This system reminds communities that they can effect change through relationships, and it helps remove emotion and fear from a community response. It has made our region safer."—James R. Pavlich, executive director of operations, Montrose County School District, Montrose, Colorado

Youth Violence Prevention

Youth Violence Prevention

The Pathway Back through Inclusion and Connection

John Van Dreal
Courtenay McCarthy
Coleen Van Dreal

ROWMAN & LITTLEFIELD
Lanham • Boulder • New York • London

Published by Rowman & Littlefield
An imprint of The Rowman & Littlefield Publishing Group, Inc.
4501 Forbes Boulevard, Suite 200, Lanham, Maryland 20706
www.rowman.com

86-90 Paul Street, London EC2A 4NE, United Kingdom

Copyright © 2022 by John Van Dreal, Courtenay McCarthy, and Coleen Van Dreal

All rights reserved. No part of this book may be reproduced in any form or by any electronic or mechanical means, including information storage and retrieval systems, without written permission from the publisher, except by a reviewer who may quote passages in a review.

British Library Cataloguing in Publication Information Available

Library of Congress Cataloging-in-Publication Data

Names: Van Dreal, John, 1962– author. | McCarthy, Courtenay, author. | Van Dreal, Coleen, author.
Title: Youth violence prevention : the pathway back through inclusion and connection / John Van Dreal, Courtenay McCarthy, Coleen Van Dreal.
Description: Lanham : Rowman & Littlefield, [2022] | Includes bibliographical references. | Summary: "This is a book about behavioral threat assessment that focuses on prevention and early intervention"—Provided by publisher.
Identifiers: LCCN 2021049966 (print) | LCCN 2021049967 (ebook) | ISBN 9781475862652 (cloth ; alk. paper) | ISBN 9781475862669 (paperback ; alk. paper) | ISBN 9781475862676 (epub)
Subjects: LCSH: School violence—United States—Prevention. | Students—Mental health—United States. | Behavioral assessment—United States. | Risk assessment—United States. | Problem youth—Education—United States. | Schools—United States—Safety measures.
Classification: LCC LB3013.32 .V36 2022 (print) | LCC LB3013.32 (ebook) | DDC 371.7/820973—dc23/eng/20211018
LC record available at https://lccn.loc.gov/2021049966
LC ebook record available at https://lccn.loc.gov/2021049967

For Lucyann, Doris, Shirley, and Janis

Contents

Foreword	xiii
Acknowledgments	xvii
Disclaimer	xxi
How This Book Is Organized, How This Book Can Help	xxiii
PART I: GETTING STARTED	1
Chapter 1: How to Build a Successful Threat Assessment Program	3
Chapter 2: Equity, Bias, and Restorative Practice: Avoiding the School-to-Prison Pipeline	29
Chapter 3: Special Education and Preventive Behavioral Threat Assessment	39
PART II: MEET THE STUDENTS	45
Chapter 4: Daniel and Will	47
Chapter 5: Alison	53
Chapter 6: Sam	59
Chapter 7: Eric and Maya	61
Chapter 8: Alan	69
PART III: BEGIN THE LEVEL 1 PROCESS	73
Chapter 9: School Site Level 1: Preventive Assessment and Intervention	75

Chapter 10: Question 12 as It Applies to the Seven Student Case
   Studies   95

Chapter 11: Questions 13–20 as They Apply to Four of the Student
   Case Studies   101

PART IV: COMPLETE THE PROCESS   111

Chapter 12: Collaborative Decision Making   113

Chapter 13: Managing Cases with Prevention, Inclusion, and
   Connection   121

Conclusion: Daniel, Will, Alison, Sam, Eric, Maya, Alan: Did It
   Work?   139

Appendix: Level 1 Team Assessment Protocolsand Forms   145

References and Resources   147

About the Authors   153

Foreword

The tragedy at Columbine High School occurred over two decades ago. It became an inflection point for responses to targeted violence in our schools and communities. Improvements in law enforcement responses and school security were implemented, as well as a wave of legislation across the country mandating a more thoughtful and strategic response to threatening behavior in schools.

While the changes in schools were well intentioned, many of the early violence prevention programs were ineffective, often relying on exclusionary policies or single-practitioner decision making that depended upon the perspective that violence happened only somewhere else. Fortunately, Salem-Keizer Public Schools, led by John Van Dreal, took a different approach, implementing the promising practice of multidisciplinary team behavioral threat assessment and management.

As a forensic psychologist who has been dedicated to violence prevention and behavioral threat assessment for over thirty years, I have always been interested in ideas, programs, and systems that employ the leading practice recommendations of experts and the anecdotal experiences of practitioners who do the work every day. When I first heard of the work John Van Dreal and his colleagues were doing in Salem, Oregon, I was hopeful that they would design and implement a functional, accessible, and efficient system of prevention and behavioral threat assessment for youths. As time passed, I enjoyed working with Van Dreal on a number of projects, including the *International Handbook of Threat Assessment, Second Edition* (Oxford, 2021) and *Making Prevention a Reality: Identifying, Assessing, and Managing the Threat of Targeted Attacks* (FBI, 2017).

While events like school shootings and other acts of targeted violence in schools are still rare, the possibility of these events occurring must be taken seriously and schools must respond with evidence-based strategies that are designed specifically for youths and youth-serving agencies. Today, the Salem-Keizer Cascade Model is an excellent example of how to proficiently assess potential youth violence while also intervening with care, empathy, and connection. As such, it has become a gold standard of violence prevention and behavioral threat assessment for school campuses and youth-serving agencies.

The authors—John Van Dreal, Courtenay McCarthy, and Coleen Van Dreal—are veterans of the safe school movement. They have over seven decades of combined experience in working directly with students, parents, education staffs, law enforcement, public mental health professionals, and several other youth-serving agencies in implementing assessment and prevention strategies.

You are about to enjoy the wisdom of their efforts. They launch their book with a powerful statement of purpose that clearly identifies their commitment to school safety, student well-being, and the use of preventive management techniques such as inclusion and building relationships. Then they provide a 40,000-foot description of the model—refreshing the memory of those who use it while also providing sufficient detail for those who are not familiar with its working elements and want to implement it within their school district or agency. They follow with insightful and informative chapters on the importance of avoiding bias, using an equity lens, utilizing restorative practice, and interacting with the special education process in both assessment and intervention.

The remainder of the book is dedicated to the human element and the art of working with people experiencing stress, trauma, and ragefully violent thinking. The authors use seven different student narratives as case studies that capture the reality of their work with a diverse student population. Within these narratives are illustrations of assessing situational elements that increase risk, and examples of avoiding stereotypes, exploring and generating prosocial resources, finding meaningful connection and mentorship, restoring trust, and using multidisciplinary decision making with a focus on prevention and inclusion.

I highly recommend this book to anyone attempting to maintain a preventive behavioral threat assessment system, as well as anyone interested in implementing a threat assessment system for a school or community. The template offered provides an excellent navigation chart for starting or refining a system, and the examples cover a broad stroke of threats and behavior types, making for excellent tabletop discussions and practice. The authors remind us that we can identify youths who are on the pathway to violence, and we can use the principles of behavioral threat assessment and the creative responses of professionals to find the pathway back to a constructive, connected life.

J. Reid Meloy, Forensic Psychologist, PhD, ABPP

Acknowledgments

First of all, we would like to thank our fellow Level 2 Investigative Team members from the Mid-Valley Student Threat Assessment Team who assisted in conducting the preventive behavioral threat assessment and management work on the cases reviewed in this book: Allan Rainwater, Becky Carpenter, Clem Spenner, Bryan Flannery, Sandy Johnson, Shelley Rutledge, Victoria Darling, and Mark Whittier.

Additionally, we would like to thank the members of the Mid-Valley Student Threat Assessment Community Team who advised and consulted: Angie Denning, Rod Swinehart, Seth Elliott, Ray Byrd, Wilson Kenney, Dave Okada, Jeff Kuhns, Ray Tuttle, Kate Kuenzi, Jeremy Wells, Robert Acosta, Jay Prall, David Zavala, Kim Dwyer, Lisa McIntyre, Trina Morgan, Peggy Morrison, Darcie Jones, Marilyn Rengert, Chris Bangs, Mike Bell, Jude McQuade-Higgins, Gail Winden, Jesse Davis, Trevor Wenning, Seantel Heisel, and Don Parise. Without the collaborative prevention work of these professionals, the cases could have ended with incarcerated or institutionalized students or, worse, severely or lethally injured victims.

The Salem-Keizer Cascade Preventive Behavioral Threat Assessment and Management System used for the assessment, prevention, support, and management of the student-involved situations reviewed in this book is the incorporation of the ideas of research experts combined with the application steps of practitioners. Many of the concepts presented have evolved through the examination and refinement of more than one expert and thus are the intellectual product of many. Where authorship is clear, citations are given. Where information has become generalized to the field of practice, references to the original source may have been missed, and so apologies are offered. As practitioners, we offer our gratitude to the following experts for their contributions to behavioral threat assessment and violence prevention.

As authors, we appreciatively note their fieldwork, research and academic contributions. Without their leadership, our work would not be possible. They are: J. Reid Meloy, William Modzeleski, Bryan Vossekuil, Katherine S. Newman, Robert A. Fein, Mary Ellen O'Toole, Eric Johnson, Gene Deisinger, Kristina Anderson, Gavin de Becker, Bob Martin, Andre Simons, James Cawood, Randy Borum, Frederick S. Calhoun, Marisa R. Randazzo, and Kris Mohandie.

The work done to build and evolve the violence prevention system used to assess, support, and manage the cases reviewed in this book was possible only through the generous leadership and support of Salem-Keizer Public Schools in Salem, Oregon; however, the ongoing tasks of maintaining the community team, deconstructing information silos, dismantling the school-to-prison pipeline, and implementing procedures that are focused on prevention and early intervention are the results of the collective efforts of the following agencies: Salem-Keizer Public Schools, Willamette Educational Services District (WESD), Marion County Sheriff's Office, Salem Police Department, Keizer Police Department, Oregon Judicial Department, Marion County Health and Human Services, Polk County Behavioral Health, Marion County Juvenile Department, Polk County Juvenile Department, Oregon Youth Authority, Marion County District Attorney's Office, Chemeketa Community College, Willamette University, and the Mid-Valley Behavioral Care Network.

The following people have contributed ideas and/or support to the Salem-Keizer Cascade System used to provide the intervention and support for the students reviewed within the case studies: Paul Keller, Ruth Gelbrich, Rich Goward, Sandy Husk, Mary Paulson, Christy Perry, Michael Wolfe, Jay Remy, Raul Ramirez, Michael Cunningham, Walt Myers, Dave Harvey, Marc Adams, Jerry Moore, John Teague, Rhonda Stueve, Cindy Poore, Mark Whittier, Pete Teller, Richard Horner, Debra Baker, Steve Kuhn, Bob Hammond, Geoff Heatherington, Dave Novotney, Linda Bonnem, Bill MacMorris-Adix, Lowell Smith, Steve Rosen, Mike McFetridge, John Troncoso, Steve Bellshaw, Craig Bazzi, Harold Burke-Sivers, Ann-Marie Bandfield, Cheri Lovre, Bud Bailey, and Dave McMullen.

We offer our heartfelt thanks to Doris Penwell, John Volbeda, Lucyann Volbeda, Shirley Swank, Janis Jones, Garritt Van Dreal, Natalie Van Dreal, George Van Dreal, Richard Swank, Little Dog, John McCarthy, and Teagan McCarthy for their support, encouragement, and dedication to our work.

To John Edmonds, our editor, we offer our apologies for the occasional mind-numbing run-on sentences and excessive capitalization, along with our admiration and gratitude for his amazing precision in catching the smallest of errors. And to Public Consulting Group and the Oklahoma State Department of Education, we offer our appreciation for their efforts in creating the online training that assisted in articulating the case studies.

A special thanks goes out to Ross Stout for keeping us organized and the Governor's Cup Coffee Roasters for providing the brain fuel required to focus on writing a book and the space to stretch out and scatter our laptops about.

A very special thanks goes to J. Reid Meloy for writing this book's foreword and his generosity, his wisdom, and his contributions to our careers.

Finally, there are many other people who have supported the implementation of our Salem-Keizer Cascade System throughout Oregon, Washington, Oklahoma, Texas, California, Idaho, Utah, New Mexico, Arizona, Colorado, Alabama, New York, Wisconsin, Michigan, Hawaii, and beyond. Hopefully, they are aware of the importance of their endorsement and efforts. If not, we offer our apologies for failing to make that point and our gratitude to them for helping to make the community a safer place.

Disclaimer

The system featured in this book is designed for the assessment of situations involving people who are engaged in activity or involved in circumstances that suggest the potential for aggression directed at other people—not for the assessment of situations involving people who are considering suicide, engaged in sexual harm, or misusing fire, unless they are doing so as part of an act of aggression intending injury to others. It is not designed to predict future violence, nor is it a foolproof method of assessing an individual's or a group's risk of harm to others. It is not a strict set of risk factors or a checklist that can be quantified or added up to total a final "score."

The student cases reviewed in this book are based on actual occurrences of potentially dangerous situations. The names, along with other details such as gender, age, and grade level, have been changed or manipulated to protect the identity of the people involved, as well as to provide clarity or example where ambiguity might have been present. When using examples in training or writing, the authors purposely avoid hyperbole or theatrics, believing that their communities and colleagues have had enough of the imagery of mass shootings and the continually promoted infamy of people who acted out their rage through violence. The cases in this book are situations (some very concerning, some not) that were addressed through a behavioral threat assessment and management process that is preventive and inclusive and that promotes positive connections. These cases were not staffed to pursue punitive measures, expulsions, or arrests (although some arrests were made and used as tools of prevention).

Further information on the Salem-Keizer Cascade Model as well as resources for violence prevention, training, consultation, and support are available at vandrealconsulting.com.

How This Book Is Organized, How This Book Can Help

Between stimulus and response there is a space. In that space is our power to choose our response. In our response lies our growth and our freedom.—Viktor E. Frankl

This is a book about prevention and early intervention. It's about thoughtful connection, inclusion, prosocial relationship building, and the restoration of meaningful and positive experiences for young people within the school environment. It's about the importance of examining potential violence through the eyes of the person considering that violence, and redirecting that person to constructive, nonviolent solutions.

This is a book about staying objective, avoiding assumptions, eliminating prejudgment, and making great effort to intervene in situations that are moving along the pathway toward violent outcome before extreme measures like arrest and institutionalization are required.

It is not a book about punitive solutions, punishment, expulsion, or exclusion. It is not about identifying the "bad kids" or using a lens that categorizes good and evil behavior. And it does not promote profiling, stereotypes, or the suspicion of someone because of race or ethnicity, socioeconomic status, gender identity, sexual orientation, or religious beliefs.

It is a book that attempts to expand the space between the stimulus of threatening behavior and the response of reactive solutions that often make situations worse, exacerbate resentment, and compel vindictive motives. As Victor Frankl so eloquently suggests in the epigraph above, that space is where we have the power to choose our response, and this book will illustrate responses and intervention plans that are focused on prosocial solutions, fortify and expand protective factors, preserve dignity, and stop a potentially violent trajectory, altering it toward healthful and safe problem-solving resolutions.

Despite considerable evidence that punishment and exclusion fail to inspire youths to become better citizens, there exist many school discipline policies, security operations, and violence prevention programs written or designed out of anger and fear resulting from school violence. These policies continue to lead to misdirected, blanket generalizations and categories that encourage extreme responses such as expulsion and arrest.

The consequence is that these measures often produce students who rarely remain detained and end up at higher risk to themselves and others, less supervised, and thus free to target potential victims. They also lead to the further disenfranchisement of those youths, accelerating potentially lifelong economic, social, and personal dysfunction.

This book is informed by interactive trainings and consultations with more than 350 school districts and youth-serving agencies and by the authors' combined 75 years of experience working with at-risk youths in schools and institutions. It is informed by evidence of the amazing changes that can result from simple interventions of inclusion, mentorship, connection, restorative practice, and care, and from the infusing of protective factors and meaningful experiences into a youth's life. Finally, it is informed by instances of extremely marginalized, troubled, and distraught students taking prosocial baby steps on a pathway back to meaningful and safe participation in schools and the community.

The book highlights a preventive behavioral threat assessment and management system and identifies the importance of using an equity lens, bias checks, trauma-informed practices, and restorative practice within the implementation and use of that system. It provides guidelines on how a preventive system functions within the rules and processes of special education and how to capitalize on a district's resources.

Following that material, the remainder of the book is dedicated to exemplifying that system by reviewing seven cases involving youths who were considering or acting out violence as a solution to their problems. You will be introduced to each student, then taken on a journey through each student's preventive behavioral threat assessment, which identifies risk factors and protective factors, then guides you to finding solutions and interventions that are pro-student, pro-safety, and inclusive and that build connections to adults and other students.

The following chapters will help you build skills that accurately identify concerns for extreme aggression, based upon an assessment of situational factors, then develop supervision and intervention strategies that are fitting to those identified concerns and thus decrease the potential for violent behavior.

Case studies will apply vetted, research-driven, leading practice assessment procedures that include equity, trauma-informed strategies, restorative practice, and bias checks (found within the Level 1 Protocol located in the appendix) to determine concerns for extreme aggression and positive, inclusive prevention strategies to de-escalate potentially violent situations.

By reviewing these cases, you will learn about the risk factors and warning signs of targeted violence and reactive aggression and how to assess threatening or inappropriate communications for indications of escalating danger, then intervene with a prevention and inclusion mindset.

This book is also a companion to *Assessing Student Threats: Implementing the Salem-Keizer System, Second Edition* (Van Dreal et al., 2017), which provides instruction on building a sustainable, community-based violence prevention and behavioral threat assessment system composed of school-site-based (Level 1) teams and a community-based (Level 2) team. That book (available at your favorite online book vendor or through bookstore order catalogs if you shop locally) provides clear procedures and user-friendly templates for a timely and effective assessment process in a manner that focuses on prevention, keeping schools safe, and continuing education opportunities for all students, including the students of concern.

This book links to that material in exemplary application, using the assessment protocol questions and intervention strategies as a template in examining the seven student situations as actual threat assessments and prevention plans. This will help you, your school site team, and multiagency team develop interventions that allow students to remain safely engaged in positive school experiences, preventing the overreliance on expulsion and arrest to resolve school safety concerns. (Examples of Salem-Keizer Cascade system forms and protocols are available through the link in the appendix.)

While this is primarily a review of case studies in assessment and intervention and is not a complete manual on implementing a preventive behavioral threat assessment and management system, readers will take away:

- An understanding of basic concepts of behavioral threat assessment.
- An understanding of leading practice recommendations for assessment, prevention, and management.
- The ability to identify the dynamics and risk factors for reactive aggression and targeted violence within K-12 schools.

- The ability to understand and identify risk factors for potential violent behavior, including those present in people who conduct mass-casualty attacks.
- A blueprint for a centralized, school district, and community-based assessment system that provides resources, assessment, and support for school site teams.
- Experience and practice in strengthening threat assessment skills and using procedures through case studies.
- Examples of equitable practices, trauma-informed strategies, and restorative practices in violence prevention.
- Examples of checkpoints that address and decrease bias in behavioral threat assessment and violence prevention.
- Examples of violence prevention methods that connect students with prosocial behavioral options and decrease student violence, decrease arrests and expulsions, and dismantle the school-to-prison pipeline.

Successful intervention leads to physically safer schools, which lead to a perception of safety and security among students and staff members. The perception of safety decreases fear, which allows the higher brain functioning needed to teach, operate a school, and learn. With an education climate that is free of serious threat or the distraction of fear, the learning experience will be far more successful and enjoyable to all students, and the work experience will be more satisfying for teachers and other staff members.

While this book focuses on specific case studies and individuals, reading it and putting its recommendations to work will ultimately have a positive effect on the school and local community.

TEST YOURSELF

1. This book is not about one of the following:
    a. Connection and prosocial relationships as goals of supervision and intervention.
    b. Arrests and/or expulsion as a goal of supervision and intervention.
    c. Inclusion as a goal of supervision and intervention.
    d. Fortifying or adding protective factors as a goal of intervention.
2. Expulsion and arrest often:
    a. Preserve the dignity of a student.
    b. Lead a youth to a more successful future.
    c. Lead to greater risk to self and others.
3. Preventive behavioral threat assessment does not utilize two of the following:

a. Identifying the profile of potentially violent students.
   b. Equity and trauma-informed practices.
   c. Bias checks and restorative practice.
   d. Access to the school-to-prison pipeline.
   e. Identification of risk factors and warning signs for targeted violence and reactive aggression.
4. This book is a companion to the book titled:
   a. *The Road*
   b. *Snapped! Case Studies in Oxygen TV Drama*
   c. *One Flew Over the Cuckoo's Nest*
   d. *Assessing Student Threats: Implementing the Salem-Keizer System*
   e. *Blood Meridian or The Evening Redness in the West*
5. This book focuses primarily on exemplifying preventive behavioral threat assessment by:
   a. Reviewing the assessment and intervention process for seven cases involving youths who were considering or acting out violence as a solution to their problems.
   b. An examination of research and leading practice recommendations for behavioral threat assessment.
   c. The use of hyperbole, hindsight narratives about well-publicized mass shootings, and traumatizing images of injured or terrorized students and teachers who are being evacuated from school shooting locations.

Answers: 1-b; 2-c; 3-a,d; 4-d; 5-a

PART I

Getting Started

Chapter 1

How to Build a Successful Threat Assessment Program

The goal of behavioral threat assessment (BTA) is to identify students in concerning situations, assess factors that indicate concern for potential violence, and identify prevention and intervention strategies to manage concerns by adding both mitigation and protective factors that connect and include the students in prosocial and meaningful experiences.

One central purpose is to differentiate between targeted and reactive aggression in the context of a student's situation. Behavioral threat assessment specifically aims to identify concerns for targeted aggression, which is aggression that includes the selection of a particular target prior to the attack (Fein et al., 1995). Targeted aggression follows a process that moves from the idea to harm another person to planning, preparation, and eventually action (Calhoun, 1998).

Reactive aggression, on the other hand, is a more common form of aggression that is temporary, does not involve pre-identified targets, and often occurs while a person is in a highly emotional state or in response to a challenge, insult, or affront (Meloy, 2000). Though the goal of BTA is the identification and management of targeted aggression, reactive aggression can also impact the physical and psychological safety of individuals in schools. For this reason, the system used as a model throughout this book also addresses the management of situations that indicate reactive aggression.

This chapter provides an overview of actionable steps that K-12 school districts can take to develop a comprehensive violence prevention plan and create processes and procedures for conducting threat assessments on their campuses.

These steps serve as minimum guidelines and might need to be adapted for a particular school's or district's unique resources and challenges. For institutions that already have prevention plans or threat assessment capabilities in place, these guidelines might provide additional information to update existing protocols or to formalize the structures of prevention, reporting, gathering information, and managing concerns for extreme aggression.

Focusing on the Salem-Keizer Cascade Model for student threat assessment, this chapter lists the sequential instructions and protocol for investigating and assessing threatening situations involving youths. The chapter also provides guidelines for conducting threat assessment through a collaborative process that involves both youth-serving and community-serving public agencies, such as K-12 education, law enforcement, public mental health services, youth parole and probation, the courts, victim advocacy, and the district attorney's office.

While this chapter does not provide data, the model is currently being reviewed by three research projects that examine referral and intervention outcomes, including impacts on underserved and at-risk populations, referral rates by race and ethnicity, and the effectiveness of preventing the school-to-prison pipeline and expulsion. One of those projects has initially found that the model supports all students with inclusion and decreases the chances of arrest and expulsion.

The model aligns with the work of Regional Education Laboratory Northwest (REL Northwest) Equity in School Discipline Collaborative to establish welcoming and safe school climates that promote equity for all students. According to REL Northwest, the model's intervention plan includes evidence-based strategies that are based on research and include the eight steps for creating a comprehensive targeted violence prevention plan outlined in the *Final Report of the Federal Commission on School Safety* (2018).

Evidence-based, culturally responsive solutions include collaboration with multidisciplinary teams, parents/guardians, and students to incorporate the values and culture of the students in the selection of solutions, ensuring communication in the language and style that accommodate the students' needs, and using data to adjust interventions as needed.

In 1999, most education policy that addressed threats and threatening behavior ranged from reactive measures to positions of complete denial. Some initial programs were well intended but ineffective in their pursuit of risk factors that were not supported by research or practice. Students frequently used threatening language, just as they do today, and educators were faced with the question of how to respond and when to treat threats as serious risks.

Many students were held out of school for days, sometimes weeks, or even expelled before they were evaluated and re-entry planning could take place, if it took place at all (Van Dreal, Cunningham, and Nishioka, 2005). Additionally, mental health practitioners became increasingly uncomfortable administering risk assessments based on psychological indicators alone.

These concerns, along with the desire to create a psychologically safe environment where teachers and students could teach and learn without the distraction of fear, motivated the development of an efficient, time-sensitive threat assessment system for youths. The project was led by Salem-Keizer Public Schools in collaboration with a team of youth-serving agencies consisting of law enforcement, juvenile justice services, county court personnel, public mental health practitioners, and child welfare services.

This collaboration was fortunate in that the school district was already a participant in a partnership with law enforcement, public health services, and juvenile justice services through a structure called the Youth Services Team (YST), which, along with the Marion County Adult Threat Advisory Team, served as a model for implementation in late fall of 2000. The collaboration was joined later by the Willamette Education Service District and is now referred to as the Salem-Keizer Cascade Model because of its broad implementation throughout Oregon and Washington.

The system was designed and refined through a thorough survey of research and leading practices recommendations in consultation with local practitioners who regularly assessed potentially violent situations involving youths. Committee work was also completed with a variety of education professionals, risk management personnel, mental health practitioners, law enforcement officers, and juvenile justice personnel.

The system has been developed to operate from a continuing quality-improvement perspective, which allows experience and new data to be incorporated into operational practices that are then updated in annual training. These updates are also included in training provided to stakeholders outside of the Salem, Oregon, area. Feedback from practitioners, educators, students, families, ongoing research, and other sources has always been an important aspect of program improvement.

The system in place today is a two-tiered prevention and intervention process that operates through assessment protocols, supervision and management consultation, and access to available community resources.

The first tier, called Level 1, is school site based and composed of administrators, counselors or other school-based mental health staff members, and sworn law enforcement officers.

The second tier, called Level 2, is community based and composed of personnel from K-12 school districts, law enforcement, public mental health services, the district attorney's office, victim advocacy, and juvenile justice.

Members of the Level 2 team are trained to the highest standards available and provide investigative assistance, assessment, consultation, and resource development directly to the schools.

Like most multiagency collaborations, the program encountered several hurdles. Foremost among the challenges were a lack of available services, differences in agency philosophies, the absence of policies to address issues regarding record sharing and confidentiality, information storage, and funding limitations. Nevertheless, each agency committed to providing support and training, and the resulting system is an example of a disciplined, collaborative problem-solving structure that has become institutional within the Mid-Willamette Valley and is being adopted throughout the Northwest and other parts of the United States.

In brief, the objectives of the system are to:

1. Identify and assess threats of potentially harmful or lethal behavior and determine the level of concern and action required.
2. Organize prevention strategies to manage situations involving students that pose threats to other students, staff members, and the community.
3. Utilize resources to avoid exclusion, keep youths in school, and improve meaningful connections with school staff members.
4. Maintain a sense of psychological safety among students, teachers, and parents, thus fostering a learning environment that allows for teaching and learning and that is free of distractions caused by fear.

The benefits of this system include:

1. Shared ownership, responsibility, and liability.
2. The inclusion of trauma-informed care, restorative practice, an inclusion perspective, and a well-rooted foundation of prevention thinking.
3. A process that has been combed to eliminate opportunities for bias and that includes protocols to check for bias.
4. A collaborative approach that allows different professional perspectives, which decreases bias, eliminates stereotyping and profiling, and stops any potential routing of students from school to prison.
5. Questions that are aligned with the recommendations of international experts and focus on situational variables, not demographic characteristics that could lead to bias.
6. An expeditious but methodical preventive assessment and intervention process.
7. Intervention that identifies and decreases high-risk situational factors while increasing protective factors, inclusion, and connection to peers and adults within the district.
8. Early intervention that leads away from the discipline system and does not support the use of exclusionary measures (both of which actually increase safety concerns in the majority of situations).

9. The identification of safety concerns in clear terms and a clarity of language that is more easily communicated to parents, teachers, and students.
10. Interventions and supervision strategies that are fitting to the situation and accurately address safety concerns (avoiding knee-jerk overreactions) and provide those involved with an accurate and realistic understanding of the problem and solutions.
11. Safety planning that keeps many students in school who otherwise would be removed through expulsion or arrest.
12. An increase in both the physical safety and the psychological safety of a school—essential to a successful learning and teaching climate for students and staff members.
13. An increase in physical and psychological safety that strengthens education and supports the teaching and learning process.
14. The inclusion of family members in the prevention and intervention process, especially before the behavior warrants adjudication or involvement of the child welfare system.

SYSTEM SPECIFICS

The two-tiered model utilizes a centralized reporting structure and examines threats of aggression, moving from assessment to management of threatening situations (at both levels) using strategies that reasonably and prudently address the risk factors and situational variables elevating the concern. It includes ongoing follow-up and reassessment to examine changing risk factors as the level of concern adjusts to the supervision and intervention.

The system is administered through a multidisciplinary, multiagency collaboration with a focus on mitigating the circumstances that exacerbate the potential for violent behavior. As such, it operates without the use of labels, myths, profiling, and overreaction. Furthermore, it has operational strategies that check implicit bias and includes the recommendation to review the local process through use of an equity lens.

The system is engaged at Level 1 when a threatening situation is detected or suspected. A threatening situation might include the communication of a direct threat, a veiled or indirect threat, the display of known risk factors for targeted violence, or an act of aggression.

Additionally, the system can be engaged to address any situation that causes concern because of the possibility of an aggressive outcome. The system is not to be used for students who are considering suicide, engaged in sexual harm, or misusing fire, unless they are doing so in combination with or as a function of an act of extreme aggression intending severe or lethal injury

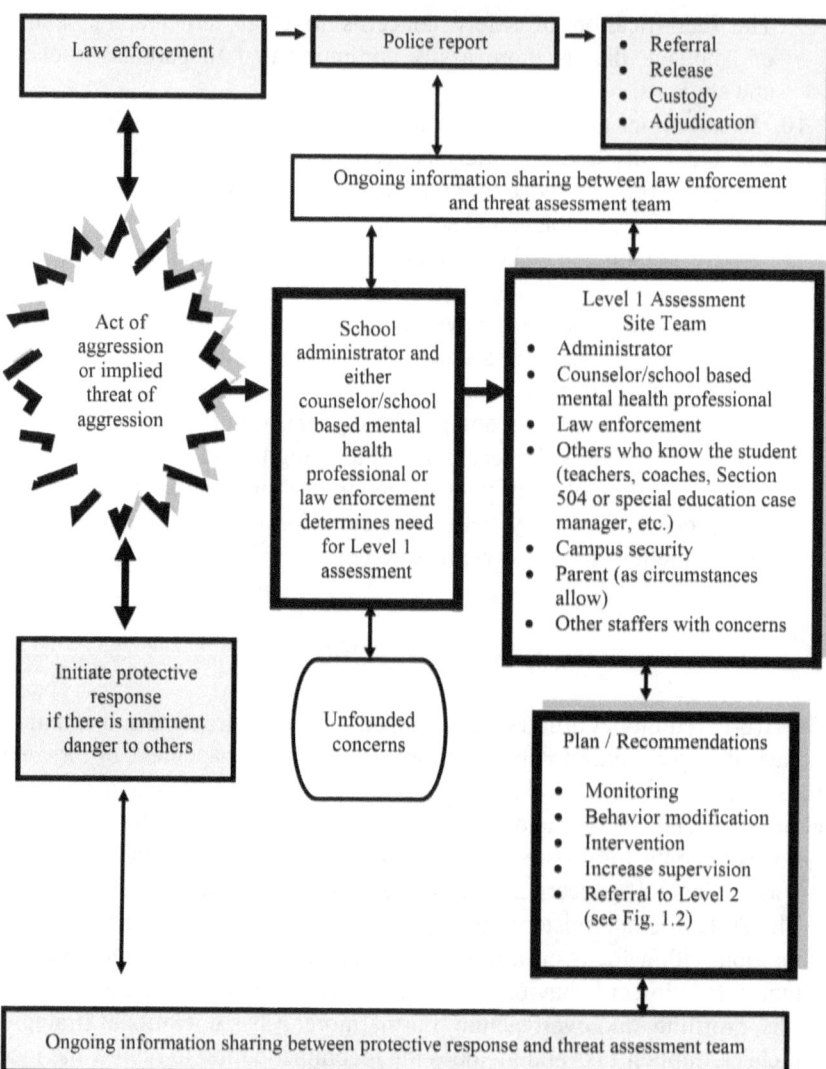

Figure 1.1.

to others. School districts should have other protocols addressing suicidal ideation, sexual harm, and fire misuse.

The system has three tracks, noted in figure 1.1.

The first track (bottom) is a protective response and occurs when imminent danger exists. In this situation, law enforcement is notified, followed by notification of the offices determined by the school district's standard operating procedures.

The second track (top) is a referral for criminal investigation when warranted and is completed by law enforcement. Depending on the sensitive nature of the investigation, information might or might not be shared with the threat assessment teams. However, as law enforcement investigates a situation, information that does not compromise the investigation but is pertinent to the threat assessment and safety planning is provided to the threat assessment team.

The investigation, in some cases, might continue as the threat assessment and management process is proceeding. However, the threat assessment and the criminal investigation should not interfere with each other.

The third track (middle) is threat assessment, initiated through a decision made by a school administrator in consultation with at least one other member of the site team. The site team is composed of an administrator, a school-based mental health professional (MHP), and a law enforcement officer trained in prevention and BTA. Members of the site team do not have to be threat assessment experts, but they do have to be trained in the use of the Level 1 process and the Level 1 assessment protocol (an example of the protocol can be found through a link in the appendix).

LEVEL 1 (SCHOOL SITE TEAM) ASSESSMENT

The Level 1 Assessment Protocol is used for the investigation and documentation of concerns regarding dangerous student activities, behaviors, ideation, and/or communications. A threat does not have to be direct or even clearly indicated to warrant a Level 1 assessment. Level 1 teams are encouraged to use the protocol to address concerns and document their review and management of potential violence, even if the concerns are dismissed as minor or unlikely.

While the Level 1 process is expeditious, it is also thorough. Many cases involving threatening communications are reactive or lack attack-related behavior and thus are assessed and managed quickly. Depending on the circumstances, the Level 1 assessment process can be brief (20–30 minutes) or lengthy (1–2 hours or more).

The Level 1 Preventive Behavioral Threat Assessment Process follows this basic sequence:

1. Determine the facts using information drawn from communications, behavior, and the specific situation of concern.
2. Take immediate actions, including notification of potential victims, to provide safety if you consider the threat to be imminent and acute.

3. Conduct an initial assessment through a multidisciplinary team process using the Level 1 protocol and any supplementary interviews or questionnaires to support fact finding.
4. Create a management plan for supervision, intervention, and prevention to address risk factors and support needs.
5. Provide team members with copies of the Level 1 management plan to assist them with their assigned prevention work.
6. Continue to assess new information, including improvements and progress, and adjust the management plan as needed.

GUIDELINES FOR CONSIDERING A LEVEL 1 ASSESSMENT

While BTA is focused on targeted violence, the likely referral flow in K-12 public education will include many referrals for reactive aggression, ongoing aggressive talk, reactive threats of violence, and bullying. To provide service and decrease the stress and anxiety of teachers, administrators, and other education staff members, a set of referral guidelines may be provided; however, these guidelines cannot be perceived as a threshold or be used to discourage referral. The Level 1 protocol provides the following suggestions for considering a referral for Level 1 assessment:

- Threat or aggression is specific to identified target with motive and plan.
- Weapon at school or attempt to bring weapon to school.
- Threat or aggression is causing considerable fear or disruption to the school environment.
- Continued intent to carry out a threat.
- History of threats of moderate to extreme aggression.
- Staff member, parent, or student perceives threatening circumstances.
- Administrator is unable to determine whether a situation poses a risk to school personnel or the community.

At times, staff members and parents might misunderstand the intention and outcome of the Level 1 assessment. Providing a disclaimer that clarifies what a threat assessment is and what it is not can be helpful. The disclaimer can and should be directed to those participating in the assessment, those receiving assessment results, and those who will be providing supervision and intervention.

It should be noted that the Level 1 assessment is not a foolproof method of assessing an individual's or a group's risk of harm to others. Ongoing observation and information gathering are necessary to mitigate potential for harm and to determine the success of intervention. The assessment does not predict future aggression, and the questions are not a checklist that can be quantified as a numerical indicator of severity. The assessment is a guide designed to identify circumstances and variables that might increase concern for potential youth aggression and to assist the school staff in the development of a management plan that addresses the issues that elevate concern.

CONDUCTING A LEVEL 1 (SITE) ASSESSMENT

1. Make sure all students and staff members are safe. If necessary, take appropriate precautions such as detaining the student of concern and restricting the student's access to coats, backpacks, lockers, phones, etc. If imminent danger exists, call law enforcement and follow the district's standard operating procedure for communication and notification.
2. Schedule the assessment as soon as the site team can assemble.
3. Using a structured threat assessment interview, the administrator (or law enforcement officer, if appropriate) interviews the student or students of concern and any witnesses to the threat or concerning behavior prior to the assessment meeting. The interview should include an examination of the threat, the situation, communications, behavior relating to a possible attack, motives, access to weaponry, accelerating factors, and protective supports. (An example of an interview is available through a link in the appendix.)
4. Use the information from these interviews to inform the Level 1 assessment, but do not include the students interviewed in the Level 1 assessment meeting.
5. Invite staff members who know the student of concern to attend the Level 1 assessment meeting. Consider teachers who have access to the student's writings or other creative work, and teachers and support staffers who know the student well. Include community agency case managers if the student is adjudicated or is a ward of the court. Include education case managers if the student is on an Individualized Education Program (IEP) or Section 504 plan. If any staff members cannot attend, provide them with a questionnaire version of the Level 1 assessment for them to complete and return before the assessment meeting. (An example of a teacher/staff questionnaire is available through a link in the appendix.) Responses from the questionnaire should be used to inform the Level 1 protocol.
6. Notify the parents or guardians that the assessment will be taking place and invite them to attend if their participation will be constructive to the assessment process. If it is determined that notification would

compromise safety or if the participation of the parent would compromise the process and/or mislead conclusions or safety decisions, the site team may elect to complete the assessment without notification and/or inclusion of the parents or guardians. However, parents or guardians should be included whenever possible. When parents or guardians do not attend the meeting (because their in-person participation might compromise the assessment or they cannot attend because of their schedules), interview them (do not ask them to fill out the form) using the Level 1 questions as a guideline. Use their responses to inform the Level 1 protocol. (An example of a parent interview is available through a link in the appendix.)

7. Meet as a team and conduct the assessment. Use a Level 1 protocol (an example is available through a link in the appendix) that includes step-by-step directions, demographics, assessment questions, intervention and supervision strategies that directly address risk factors, and instructions for further assessment through the Level 2 process. Use the Level 1 questions to guide conversation, allowing full exploration of the context and situational elements of the concern. Include information from the interview conducted with the student or students of concern and any student witnesses, as well as the information transferred from any interviews with parents or guardians (if they are not present at the assessment meeting) and any teacher questionnaires, if obtained. Include other collateral information. Be sure to scrutinize all information, including corroborating information and the motivation of the person or persons reporting, and establish facts.

8. After the questions are completed, consider the following through further discussion:
   - Were any responses based on stereotypes or assumptions rather than on actual observation and factual information regarding behavior? Are there concerning behaviors that could be appropriate within the student's culture?
   - Highlight and identify responses that indicate concern or risk.
   - Identify impressions and sense of urgency.
   - Is the potential aggression likely to cause severe or lethal injury?
   - Do the responses identify a threat that is focused on a specific target (individual or group) for a specific reason or motive and involve planning and preparation?
   - Is there a capacity to carry out the threat?
   - Is there an indication that an attack has been scheduled or an identified date when an attack might happen?
   - Is targeted violence indicated?

9. Take immediate precautionary steps to protect potential victims and assure supervision for the student or students of concern if any of the following three are true:
   - Targeted violence is indicated.
   - Potential victims are identified.
   - The potential outcome of the aggression (whether targeted or reactive) might cause severe or lethal injury.
10. Precautionary steps might include but are not limited to:
    - Calling law enforcement (911) if concern is imminent or if anyone is in immediate danger.
    - Notifying school district administrators and security personnel as outlined in district standard operating procedures.
    - Initiating a protective security response, which might include posting officers or locking or controlling all access to the school.
    - Contacting Level 2 team (community team) for further assessment, consultation, and support.
11. If targeted violence is indicated, notify the guardians of the potential target(s). Provide them with your concerns and the actions you are initiating. Document all communication with parents or guardians, develop a safety plan for the targeted student(s), and make appropriate referrals to community resources, such as victim advocacy, when appropriate. (An example of a safety plan is available through a link in the appendix.)
12. Evaluate all options available to decrease the chances of violence. While options might include restricting access to the target(s) or the school campus, removing any students who pose a threat does not necessarily decrease the threat if the students are unsupervised when away from campus. Therefore, since the use of expulsion or exclusion might create another grievance, decrease supervision, and increase concern, the elevated risk that might result should be considered before that decision is made.
13. Use fair, reasonable, and adequate supervision strategies and interventions to address the concerns and aggravating factors identified through the assessment process. Supervision strategies should be unique to each student based on situational factors. (An example of an intervention menu can be found on the Level 1 protocol located through a link in the appendix.) Be sure to monitor and factor the responses of the student of concern into further assessment if necessary.
14. Determine whether further assessment and support are needed. If so, refer to the Level 2 team. The following criteria can guide the Level 1 team in that decision:

- Your team has concerns regarding extreme aggression but is unable to confidently answer the questions from chapters 9–11 (from the Level 1 assessment protocol).
- Your team confidently answered the questions from chapters 9–11 (from the Level 1 assessment protocol) and has safety concerns regarding impulsive or reactive behavior that will likely result in serious or lethal injury to another.
- Your team has confidently answered the questions from chapters 9–11 (from the Level 1 assessment protocol) and has concerns regarding threats of targeted aggression that indicate motive, plan, preparation, scheduling, and/or other behavior that suggests the serious consideration of an act of targeted aggression.
- Your team has exhausted its building resources and would like to explore community support to assist with intervention, management, and supervision.
- A student has brought a gun to school, attempted to acquire a gun with intent to harm or intimidate others, or has been arrested for firearm-related offenses in the community.

WHAT ARE THE UNIQUE NEEDS OF YOUR SITE-BASED LEVEL 1 PROCESS?

- FTE: How is your school staffed? Do you have school counselors or other assigned mental health professionals who can sit on your Level 1 teams? If not, consider training a lead teacher, a special education teacher, or another staffer who has a professional understanding of mental health issues and disabilities to be a team member. Additionally, if your school district does not have a contract or memorandum of agreement with law enforcement for school-related partnership (such as a school resource officer program or child protective investigations), consider engaging the police chief or sheriff to collaborate on providing officers trained in preventive BTA to consult and advise schools on Level 1 cases. The teaming can be done in an in-person meeting, a conference call, or an online meeting.
- Resources: Identify your school and community resources available for intervention and supervision. Add these to step 4 if they are not already reflected within the options. If your school is short of resources, conduct a meeting to brainstorm inexpensive or even free alternatives, such as mentorship programs, use of volunteers, and potential scholarships or grants (as available from state or federal agencies as well as commercial institutions).

- Equity: Use an equity lens to examine the effects of the system on minoritized or underserved populations within your community. Engage in this review to mitigate unintended consequences or potential barriers to success (see chapter 2 for more information on this topic).
- Time: Level 1 assessment meetings can take from 20 to 90 minutes, depending on the severity and urgency of the situation. Training, practice, and preparation (with information regarding risk factors) will allow you to conduct efficient and focused meetings. Know the material, know the process, and stay focused on prevention, behavior, and situational variables.
- Training: When hired, new administrators, school-based mental health professionals, and law enforcement officers who will participate on your Level 1 teams should be trained in the use of the system and the nature of the questions. Those previously trained should be provided with ongoing refresher courses.
- Frequency of meetings: Doing threat assessment work will make you better at identifying important risk factors and prevention strategies as well as moving a meeting along with efficiency. If you do not have frequent cases to assess, consider setting up a 30-minute meeting once every two weeks to discuss fictional cases (or those highlighted by this book) and review Level 1 questions as they would apply.

CONDUCTING A LEVEL 2 (COMMUNITY TEAM) ASSESSMENT

The Level 2 team, or Student Threat Assessment Team (STAT), is composed of professionals from school districts and other education institutions, law enforcement, public mental health services, juvenile justice, the state youth authority, the district attorney's office, and victim advocacy. Following a multidisciplinary process, the collaboration (figure 1.2) is a community-based consultation team that assesses situations of concern for violence and supports schools with solutions, resource exploration, and supervision planning.

The team does not mandate interventions and does not have the authority to bypass or override policy or procedure, including special education and Section 504, of any agency or institution. While the Level 2 team shares in the responsibility of school and community safety, the school or agency Level 1 team maintains the case management, authority, and responsibility for final decisions about intervention and supervision.

A Level 2 assessment is conducted primarily at the school site by an investigative team (figure 1.2). The investigative team represents the entire Level 2 team membership and is composed of three primary members, all trained

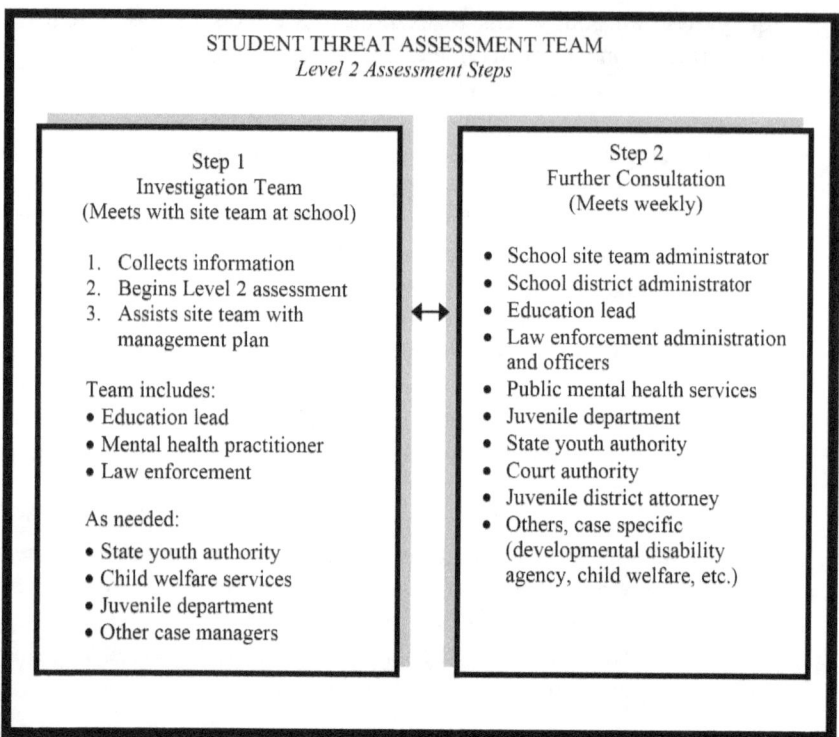

Figure 1.2.

in advanced threat assessment and management (Fein, Vossekuil, Pollack, Borum, Modzeleski, and Reddy, 2002).

The lead is an education professional, usually a school psychologist or education specialist. The second investigative team member is a public mental health worker, and the third member is a law enforcement officer. Other Level 2 team members may be included in the investigative team as appropriate to the case (such as a juvenile probation officer, a state youth authority worker, or a child welfare services case manager).

The three primary members of the investigative team complete their investigation using protocols tailored to each of their professional perspectives. Protocol questions reflect the questions found within the Level 1 process but include deeper investigation and further inquiry about social functioning, educational functioning, family systems, and personal risk factors. (Examples of Level 2 assessment protocols can be located through a link in the appendix.)

As a threat assessment investigative team, they maintain ongoing communication and consultation with the Level 2 members of the greater team as needed. They conduct the bulk of the Level 2 investigation through meetings and interviews with school staff members, parents, and other sources of information. While this is done most efficiently in one meeting, there are times when separate meetings are necessary to focus on one source of information.

The following are the specifics regarding the roles of each member of the investigative team.

EDUCATION

The majority of student threat assessments are done through school connections and most often at a school site. In fact, even if an assessment is initiated through another team agency, such as the juvenile department or law enforcement, the bulk of the work and investigation usually takes place using school resources and information. Furthermore, since the schools house and supervise youths for a large portion of their waking day, education staffers take the lead in organizing and implementing the threat assessment system.

The lead position coordinates the assessment process and organizes materials, records, and protocols. The lead is responsible for interpreting the world of education to the other members of the team and is someone who has well-established, positive relationships with other educators. The lead should be well versed in the rules, policies, and culture of education with a strong understanding of school discipline, psychoeducational assessment and diagnostics, special education, and administrative rules and procedures.

From this perspective, the lead will have the confidence and ability to provide ongoing support and follow-up assessment as well as the articulation of the limitations within the school system, the rules, and even the politics that can be a subtext to some of the decisions or resource restrictions. Having a clear understanding of what will or will not work within the school setting will greatly affect a team's ability to provide management strategies that are most appropriate to the situation.

The lead reviews the records, circumstantial information, Level 1 information, and preliminary interviews with the student or students of concern, administrators, school staff members, parents, and other available sources. The accumulated information is then discussed through further assessment and inquiry within the Level 2 investigation meeting, along with the coordinated investigations of the team's MHP and law enforcement officer.

As the information is reviewed, the team generates intervention and supervision recommendations that best address the risk factors that elevate concern and then explores resources and safety options that support both the student or students of concern and the school.

As the team concludes the initial phase of the assessment, the lead coordinates the information and prepares to present it to the greater Level 2 team at a predesignated or scheduled meeting.

MENTAL HEALTH

As a member of the investigative team, the MHP analyzes the threat and the behavior from a clinical perspective, provides an understanding of clinical diagnosis and mental health issues, and translates technical psychiatric language to members of the team. However, as opposed to a traditional practitioner and diagnostic model, the mental health role "articulates behavioral patterns, translates behavior in the context of assessing violence potential, and develops strategies to manage and contain potentially violent behavior instead of authoring treatment plans" (Gelles, Sasaki-Swindle, and Palarea, 2002).

The MHP role provides consultation, not clinical evaluation or treatment. The MHP also might conduct a mental health evaluation that further examines the impact of mental health issues on an increased concern of violence; however, this would be in addition to the consultation provided through the team. If a need for mental health evaluation is indicated, the evaluation is done through interviews with the student, family, and school staff.

The results of the evaluation will provide further examination of the student's mental health condition or other motivation in making the threat or behaving in a threatening manner. This is especially beneficial where there are clear mental health issues or when there is a need to correct the often misguided public perception that only "crazy people" make threats (Van Dreal et al., 2017). The evaluation also can assist in determining needs for mental health interventions or hospitalization.

Regardless of the possible mental health evaluation work, the primary responsibility of the MHP is to support the investigation by translating the behavior and communication of the student or students of concern (Gelles, Sasaki-Swindle, and Palarea, 2002). As a consultant, the MHP assists the team in examining resources and interventions that focus on the safety of the student of concern as well as the potential victims. The MHP role broadens the team partnership and is an essential part of the comprehensive assessment (Fein et al., 2002).

As a key member of the team, the MHP should provide (Van Dreal et al., 2017):

- An understanding of clinical diagnosis and mental health issues, as well as an ability to translate technical psychiatric language to members of the team.
- Mental health evaluation skills and an understanding of the evaluation options within the community.
- In-depth mental health assessments from a threat assessment perspective when requested.
- A functional awareness and understanding of local mental health systems and access options such as immediate hospitalization, counseling services, indigent services, crisis assessment options, long-term hospitalization, respite, and in-school resources.
- A process perspective and an appreciation for the unique perspectives of officials within the education system and law enforcement.

The investigation process for the MHP is informed by collaborative decision making and sometimes through an empirically guided assessment protocol, combined with the careful observation of the risk factors for targeted violence. The MHP is well trained in threat assessment, experienced in behavioral assessment, well versed in working with law enforcement investigation, and skilled in crisis intervention.

LAW ENFORCEMENT

The Safe School Initiative (Vossekuil et al., 2002) identified law enforcement as a primary participant in school threat assessment. The Salem-Keizer Cascade Model fully supports this recommendation. As members of both the Level 1 and Level 2 threat assessment teams, law enforcement officers are trained to understand prevention and the unique requirements and challenges of BTA. Team members rely on law enforcement officers to provide an in-depth law enforcement perspective and specialized assessment, taking into consideration targeted violence risk factors, intervention options, threat management, and insight regarding criminal behavior (NASP, 2020).

In a Level 2 assessment, the officer, working directly with the education lead and the public mental health lead, takes an active role in the investigation. The officer employs available law enforcement investigative skills and resources to gather in-depth information regarding the situation, the context, and the student or students of concern. The officer also might gather extra information about inhibitors and other support systems, triggers, family dynamics, perceived alternatives to violence, and motive.

Threat assessments are not criminal investigations (though a criminal investigation might occur alongside a threat assessment), so the law enforcement officer must use different strategies and perspectives than a standard police investigation. Law enforcement officers do bring a familiarity with the criminal justice system and the impact and processes of custody (both criminal and protective) and criminal prosecution. They will have knowledge of and perspective on dynamics within the community in which the student resides and can be a source of information about community-based programs and other resources available to the team.

The officer combines law enforcement and threat assessment knowledge with an early intervention perspective, an understanding of child development and trauma-informed practices, and culturally responsive intervention, to participate collectively with the team in assessing and preventing a threatening situation, even in circumstances that might not include illegal behavior.

Multidisciplinary threat assessment is a prevention-based model, and though often a crime has not been committed, making efforts to address the situation can prevent an act of violence. The following tasks are features of the law enforcement Level 2 investigation:

- Examining the implications of arrest or other disciplinary actions on a student's situation.
- Considering short- and long-term management strategies that reduce the concern.
- Identifying how a person who poses a threat, but has not yet committed a crime, might be in need of intervention and management and does not simply become a problem for another person or agency.
- Gathering information on and noting the significance of attack-related behavior (plans for violent action, target identification and research, preparation, rehearsal, and approach behavior).
- Noting suicidality.
- Noting alternatives to violence.
- Conducting criminal history checks of the involved parties.
- Querying police contacts in the community.
- Conducting home visits, including search and seizure when necessary.
- Making arrests as a last resort when necessary.
- Taking protective action when necessary.
- Providing knowledge of and familiarity with the criminal justice system, as well as unique law enforcement-related resources such as surveillance of subjects and crime prevention services.
- Conducting interviews and background inquiries and scrutinizing behavioral patterns.
- Analyzing telephone data, electronic media, social media, and forensic evidence from both a criminal and threat assessment perspective.

The law enforcement officer compiles pertinent information and presents it to the threat assessment team. This information can be instrumental in the overall assessment and the subsequent development of management strategies in threat assessment cases. All members of the team then work objectively to apply knowledge and experience in their collaborative assessment of a situation.

As a result, some of the management plans might be unconventional in the eyes of traditional law enforcement. Management plans and interventions might employ subtle actions, such as reinforcing social and emotional support systems, building mentorships and connections within the school and community, and introducing or enhancing protective factors (also referred to as inhibitors).

OTHER AGENCY INVOLVEMENT

In addition to educators, law enforcement officers, public mental health officials, and the other agencies listed in figure 1.2, there are other youth-serving agencies that assist in and consult on the Level 2 team. Child welfare services, disability services, and other community-based youth service agencies might sit on the team and provide perspectives on concern for aggressive behavior, threat management, and community resources.

Furthermore, with adjudicated youths, these agencies can offer considerable assistance with planning and supervision options. Different schools and communities might identify other partners not listed here, and the members of their teams might vary based on the dynamics of their community.

LEVEL 2 COMMUNITY TEAM MEETING OR STAT

The investigative team is the outreach component of the Level 2 community team. As such, it does the bulk of the assessment. After the investigative team completes the assessment and consults on management strategies, the case is scheduled for further Level 2 review with the community team. The school administrator and possibly other members of the Level 1 site team will usually attend either in person or by conference call and, along with the investigative team, present the case in summary.

The community team will then conduct further assessment if needed and advise on concern for aggression, management and intervention strategies, and community resources, and will assist in building a plan for continued school support and follow-up.

The Level 2 community team meets weekly (or more often if needed) and reviews cases using the following format and guidelines.

FORMAT

- Up to 10 minutes: Case manager (school administrator or counselor, agency case worker, and/or law enforcement officer) reviews threat or incident, concerns, and the supervision and intervention currently in place.
- Up to 15 minutes: Investigative team presents results of assessment.
- Up to 20 minutes: Community team conducts further assessment, consults on supervision strategies, and explores community resources.

The Level 2 community team meets on a regular basis (weekly, if possible) and addresses all new cases as well as follow-up information from past cases. The group functions as a consultation team and focuses on the assessment of situations that pose concern for a violent outcome. Since the community team relies on its participating agencies' time and commitment, team members must be well trained, invested in the work, and aware of the time limitations in order to establish a well-functioning and efficient process that balances assessment with the exploration of resource options and management.

The Level 2 community team advises on the frequency of follow-up investigation, reviews the cases as determined, and provides consultation as circumstances change and/or as supervision needs increase. Because threatening situations are fluid and vary with intervention and supervision changes, a case may be reviewed and reassessed at any time on the request of the site team.

Those involved in the supervision and intervention retain copies of recommendations (including the Level 1 recommendations) as references from which to work. Official copies of threat assessment documents are maintained in an envelope marked confidential and are stored in a student's cumulative file, with a second copy housed in a central location, such as the security office, student services department, or district-level administration office.

The student threat assessment system is maintained through the coordinating efforts of the education lead (a single point of contact), who tracks all training, assessment, intervention, and follow-up and monitors the process for fidelity.

Threat assessments and prevention work are fluid. Once the risk factors are identified and then addressed through prevention and intervention strategies, success can be identified through informal staffing and conversations with parents, teachers, the student, and other school personnel.

As items from the management plan are completed and behavior has stabilized, the case manager administrator, in consultation with other members of the Level 1 team, might decide that the situation no longer poses a risk of extreme aggression and can be retired. The decision is noted, along with the reasons for retiring the case, in the review notes at the end of the Level 1 form.

The system is protocol driven and user friendly, catering to the culture and needs of the K-12 education environment. However, the model has been adapted to serve community colleges and other higher education institutions.

While it is impossible to measure events that have not occurred, it is possible to measure the impressions of those who have used the Salem-Keizer Cascade Model. In a study completed by the University of Oregon's Institute on Violence and Destructive Behavior (Van Dreal, Cunningham, and Nishioka, 2005), 95% of administrators and counselors using the model stated that the system effectively identified potentially dangerous students and situations, had positive effects on school safety, and provided important information necessary for support, discipline, and placement decisions.

The same study found that 90% of administrators reported that the system improved efficient coordination with law enforcement and mental health practitioners. Overall, school administrators and counselors strongly endorsed the system. The vast majority of respondents believed that the system was an important and valuable part of maintaining safety in schools and provided support for referred students.

WHAT ARE THE UNIQUE NEEDS OF YOUR LEVEL 2 COMMUNITY TEAM?

- Staffing (FTE): What are your district's or organization's personnel options? Do you have a position that can be dedicated to implementing and piloting this system? Consider approximately 1 FTE (full-time equivalent) for every 40,000 students. If fewer students, the responsibilities can be paired with other work or written into an existing job description as a part-time feature. For example, in a small district, a student services program assistant may coordinate a district's prevention programs, parent complaints, and equity, and chair the BTA system.
- Resources: What kind of community supports exist? Are there public health employees who can contribute time, support, and counsel to the team? Are there other youth-serving agencies that can contribute time and support? Does your community have extracurricular activities available to youths, and, if so, are there grants or scholarships available? Consider exploring state, regional, and national grants to create resources or to fund counseling and other activities for at-risk youths.

Keep in mind that the primary goal is to decrease risk by keeping kids busy and connecting them with prosocial adults.
- Distance: How large is your district or region of operation? Will team member travel be an issue? With the success of online meeting platforms like Teams and Zoom, in-person attendance is much less of an issue.
- Training: Level 2 community teams require initial training and ongoing refresher courses. Additionally, prevention and assessment training provided by experts can be very helpful in honing and refining skills. The Association of Threat Assessment Professionals (ATAP) is an international organization that provides excellent training, networking, and professional associations on an ongoing basis. Membership requirements and options can be found at www.atapworldwide.org.
- Frequency of meetings: As noted above, for a district of 40,000 students, consider at least 60 minutes a week for Level 2 community team meetings. Frequency is important because doing the work improves skills. Even if there are no new cases, a Level 2 community team should meet regularly (every week, if possible) to discuss past cases, follow up, and perhaps do tabletop case studies. This creates a more fluid and expert team, builds relationships and trust within and between agencies, and supports the goal of prevention rather than reaction.
- Availability: Level 2 community team members are essential to the success of this model. Both field workers and administrators should attend meetings on a regular basis.
- Agency commitment: Use of a basic MOU (memorandum of understanding), an MOA (memorandum of agreement), or an IGA (intergovernmental agreement) can provide written commitment and outline expectations for membership on the team. (An example of a basic MOU is provided through a link in the appendix.)
- Choosing team members: The following is a list of traits and skills necessary to function successfully on a Level 2 community preventive BTA team (from The Safe School Initiative):
  1. An ability to relate well to others (staff members, colleagues, other professionals, students, parents, and the public).
  2. An awareness of and sensitivity to the difference between harming and helping in an intervention.
  3. A reputation for fairness and trustworthiness (throughout the community of agencies that serve youths as well as the community as a whole).
  4. A questioning, analytical, and even skeptical mindset.
  5. Training in the collection and evaluation of information from multiple sources. An ability to "investigate."

6. Discretion and an appreciation for the importance of keeping information confidential and an understanding of the possible harm that might result in the inappropriate release of information.
7. Familiarity with the contemporary issues of school and community safety.
8. The ability to serve as a formal link or liaison between various systems and meet regularly within those systems (a "boundary spanner" who believes in the project and process).
9. In-depth knowledge about the team member's own organization, resource availability, and both political and ethical boundaries.
10. Someone who can speak to the agency's commitment and decision process as well as to his or her contribution.
11. Credibility, respect, and strong interpersonal skills.
12. A member who is supported by his or her agency's administration.

This chapter provides an overview of actionable steps that K-12 school districts can take to develop a comprehensive violence prevention plan and create processes and procedures for conducting threat assessments on their campuses. For institutions that already have prevention plans or threat assessment capabilities in place, these guidelines might provide additional information to update existing protocols or to formalize the assessment and management of potential aggression.

For more information or detail on the implementation of the Salem-Keizer Cascade Model, see the references and resources section of this book or visit www.vandrealconsulting.com.

TEST YOURSELF

1. One objective of the Salem-Keizer Cascade Model of BTA is to:
   a. Harden any potential soft targets through fencing, metal detectors, etc.
   b. Make forecasts, predictions, and profiles that determine whether an individual will actually carry out targeted violence.
   c. Assess the level of concern of potentially harmful and lethal behavior.
   d. Provide a map and a plan for hiking one of the country's most glorious mountain ranges.
2. The Level 1 Threat Assessment Protocol is designed for:
   a. A school site team that consists of at least an administrator, a school-based MHP, and a law enforcement officer.
   b. A collaborative community team that consists of representatives from community agencies associated with education, mental health, law enforcement, juvenile justice, etc.

c. A teacher or faculty member to complete as a questionnaire about a student of concern.
3. Two important areas of focus of preventive BTA and management are:
   a. Building prosocial connections and relationships and making considerable efforts to keep a student of concern in a school setting.
   b. Surveillance systems that use the latest technology.
   c. Zero tolerance.
   d. Strengthening and adding protective factors for students of concern.
4. The Salem-Keizer Cascade Model is designed to focus on:
   a. Capturing, detaining, and arresting potential school shooters.
   b. Identifying the profiles of violent students so they can be handled correctly and schools can add the security measures necessary to harden the target.
   c. Identifying risk factors so prevention and early intervention can be used to deter potentially violent or aggressive situations.
5. Two of the following are reasons to initiate a Level 1 assessment:
   a. Teachers do not like working with a student because he disrupts class with jokes and off-color comments about political leaders.
   b. There is a history of threats, aggression, or violence.
   c. A parent told you that the student looks like a school shooter.
   d. A threat, aggression, or violence is specific to an identified target with motive and plan.
   e. A student fits a profile description from the latest Netflix series on serial killers.
   f. You are building a case for expulsion.
   g. You are hoping to get the student on an IEP.
   h. Pressure from the parents because they want to place their child in foster care.
   i. A student's parents have voted for a presidential candidate you don't like.
   j. You are worried that a student will vandalize the school.
6. To implement the Level 1 system effectively:
   a. Ask the police to take over the process.
   b. Ask the health department to take over the process.
   c. Evaluate your resources, staff availability, and time availability.
   d. Consider referring all students who make threats to mental health providers.
7. Which one of the following is not part of the Level 1 preventive BTA process?
   a. Take immediate actions, including notification of potential victims, to provide safety if you consider the threat to be imminent and acute.

b. Conduct initial assessment through a multidisciplinary team process using the Level 1 protocol and any supplementary interviews or questionnaires to support fact finding.
   c. Pursue an arrest or expulsion to remove the student from the school so that staff members and students will be safer.
   d. Create a management plan for supervision, intervention, and a prevention plan to address risk factors and support needs.
8. As you implement the Level 1 system in your district, each school should identify the following team members for training:
   a. A teacher, an instructional assistant, and an SRO/law enforcement support.
   b. An administrator, an SRO/law enforcement support, and an instructional assistant.
   c. An administrator, a school-based MHP, and a law enforcement officer.
   d. A member of the school board, an administrator, and Joe Exotic, The Tiger King.
9. A Level 1 assessment should be completed by:
   a. Just an administrator.
   b. The parent and an attorney.
   c. A trained school team consisting of at least an administrator, a school-based MHP, and a law enforcement officer.
   d. The team from CSI Las Vegas.

10. A Level 2 assessment is conducted primarily at the school site by an investigative team that represents the entire Level 2 team membership and is composed of:

a. An attorney, a police detective, and a psychiatrist.
b. Three primary members (an educator, a public MHP, and a law enforcement officer), all trained in advanced threat assessment and management.
c. Specialists who have an expertise in surveillance.

Answers: 1-c; 2-a; 3-a,d; 4-c; 5-b,d; 6-c; 7-c; 8-c; 9-c

Chapter 2

Equity, Bias, and Restorative Practice

Avoiding the School-to-Prison Pipeline

All humans are capable of violent behavior, given a motive that is personally compelling, a means to act out, and a lack of restraining circumstances. You have only to imagine someone trying to injure or kill you or someone you love, and you can quickly justify brutal, if not lethal, actions on your part to prevent or mitigate the harm. With that in mind, as noted earlier in this book, conducting preventive behavioral threat assessment and management is simply examining behavioral and contextual indicators that suggest someone is considering or even planning an act of violence.

Behavioral threat assessment is not about predicting behavior based on culture, religion, race, ethnicity, physical attributes, clothing, sexual orientation, gender identity, or any other aspect of identity. While people who have been bullied because of their appearance or identity sometimes act out in revenge, those who are resentful for other reasons are equally capable of doing so.

If the motive is great enough to lead to an act of violence, behavioral threat assessment is about determining risk factors that accelerate that motive and then eliminating or decreasing those risk factors. The examination of culture, race, ethnicity, and other features of identity is important in context, but the potential for violence based on such attributes should not be factored into the risk assessment.

Examining and understanding a student's unique identification or attachment to a group are most important during the steps of intervention and management because intervention strategies should be culturally responsive and address any needed supports that will increase connection and engagement. It is also important in identifying groups that might be less trusting of the institution of education and thus will need additional or different resources for building bridges of confidence and collaboration.

Though behavioral threat assessment is ideally free from profiling and stereotyping, a system can stray from its original intention and design without the ongoing provision of high-quality training, responsible program management and evaluation, and the frequent assessment of fidelity. This chapter will address equity, bias and bias mitigation strategies, and the use of restorative practices in student behavioral threat assessment to promote positive, supportive outcomes and to avoid contributing to the school-to-prison pipeline.

EQUITY

One essential component of both program initiation and ongoing management is ensuring that the system provides equitable outcomes for all students and that barriers to success are eliminated. When developing or maintaining a system, use an equity lens to assess the impact of the process on underserved or minoritized populations.

Consider meeting with the community-based threat assessment team and other district and community stakeholders to engage in an objective conversation about the threat assessment system using the following guiding questions or the equity lens that is used in your community. The following are a verbatim sampling of questions that are currently used by the Salem-Keizer School Board (2017) and the Oregon Education Investment Board (2014):

- Does the initiative align with the district's mission and values?
- Who are the racial/ethnic and underserved groups affected? What is the potential impact of the resource allocation and strategic investments on those groups?
- Does the decision being made ignore or worsen existing disparities or produce other unintended consequences? What is the impact on eliminating the opportunity gap?
- Have there been unintended consequences affecting equity because of this decision, and how have those unintended consequences been mitigated?
- What are the barriers to more equitable outcomes (e.g., mandated, political, emotional, financial, programmatic, or managerial)?
- How have members of the community been intentionally involved in the decision-making process? What do those people tell us about the proposal that has resulted?
- How does this decision build capacity or power in underserved groups?
- How are you collecting data on race, ethnicity, and native languages?
- What do the data show about the success of subgroups due to this decision?

After a collaborative examination of equity, determine how your system will mitigate any potential unintended consequences and how you will collect data to engage in ongoing equity reviews. Research on the Comprehensive Student Threat Assessment Guidelines, which is a system quite similar in structure to the Salem-Keizer Cascade Model, provides an example of the type of data that may be collected. Data were collected on discipline of students involved in threat assessment cases and showed no disparity in outcomes based on race or ethnicity (Cornell and Maeng, 2018), which is significant because overrepresentation of students of color in exclusionary discipline practices nationally is a significant concern.

BIAS

Any assessment process has the potential for unintended bias. Those engaging in behavioral threat assessment must have a thorough understanding of bias and how to mitigate the potential for bias to enter into assessment and management decisions.

A type of bias that affects all systems is implicit bias. Implicit bias is defined as the "attitudes or stereotypes (beliefs) that affect our understanding, actions, and decisions in an unconscious manner" (Kirwan Institute, 2021). Implicit bias can come into play during all phases of the assessment and management process, including reporting, information gathering, assessment, and management planning.

Strategies that can combat this type of bias include scrutinizing referral/information sources and the motivations for reports to establish verifiable facts. For example, teams should engage in planful, culturally sensitive information gathering and consider a student's background to determine who might be the most appropriate interviewer.

Teams should include or consult with a person from the same cultural background as the student being assessed in order to gain perspective on whether the behavior of concern might be appropriate within the student's culture and to aid in the provision of culturally responsive intervention strategies.

Additional types of bias that have the potential to affect the threat assessment process were identified by the Federal Bureau of Investigation (FBI, 2015) and Mary Ellen O'Toole (2014) and include the following:

- Confirmation bias—the tendency to look for evidence or interpret information in a way that confirms a preconceived opinion. This tends to be the most common and problematic type of bias in behavioral threat assessment because it causes people to notice and seek out information that supports their beliefs, ignore information that contradicts their

beliefs, and accept information that supports their preconceived notions at face value. Confirmation bias also allows a faster and easier recollection of information that is skewed to confirm a belief.
- Availability bias—the tendency to assign the most importance to behavior that comes immediately to mind, often that which is most recent. Teams can fall prey to this type of bias by focusing only on recent information and dismissing or ignoring older information when engaging in ongoing assessment. It is important to evaluate behavior over time and remind team members of the entirety of case events when engaging in ongoing assessment.
- Hindsight bias—the inclination to see past events as being more predictable than they actually were. When an intervention is unsuccessful or a student with an active management plan acts out aggressively, team members might erroneously believe that the outcome was predictable and might become disillusioned with the process.
- Foresight bias—the tendency to overestimate the ability to predict events. It is crucial for those involved in behavioral threat assessment to understand that targeted violence is not predictable but is preventable. Teams must have this understanding and assess only the facts at hand, rather than making predictions or engaging in "what if" thinking. In addition, foresight bias could prompt team members to conclude that cases with some similarity will have the same outcome or will benefit from the same interventions and thus lose sight of the unique nature of each situation.
- Normalcy bias—the tendency to attempt to find a normal explanation for behavior or dismiss concerns because an event has never occurred before, or a belief that it "could never happen here." Training staff members, students, parents, and community members to report all threatening behavior, regardless of their appraisal of the situation, can mitigate this type of bias.
- Icon intimidation or influence—the perspective that a person in a position of power or influence could not be capable of dangerous behavior. This can occur in schools with popular students, athletes, academically successful students, students from affluent families, etc.

It's important to be aware of bias in the threat assessment processes so that it can be managed, and to allow the assessment to lead to positive and equitable outcomes. The multidisciplinary process itself is a buffer against bias, because people with varied professional perspectives and life experiences are able to check the biases of others and develop better conclusions than any single person.

Consistently using a multidisciplinary structure during decision making or assessment is a powerful bias mitigation strategy. In addition, encourage team members to openly share their perspectives, even when it conflicts with the opinion of the majority, and choose team members who are comfortable sharing their perspectives.

All team members should receive training in the various types of bias and mitigation strategies. Teams are more likely to display bias in long-term or unusually intense cases where fatigue or complacency becomes a concern. Promoting self-care strategies, managing fatigue, and attempting to promote a positive mental outlook among team members can help alleviate bias in these situations.

The Level 1 protocol contains opportunities for teams to have a collaborative discussion on the potential for bias during the assessment process. The questions to be asked include: Were any responses based on stereotypes or assumptions rather than on actual observation and factual information regarding behavior? Are there concerning behaviors that could be appropriate within the student's culture? A thoughtful examination of these questions through collaborative dialogue leads to a greater likelihood that potential biases will be addressed and that team members will have the opportunity to express any concerns about the impact of bias in the process.

RESTORATIVE PRACTICES

Restorative practices (derived from the term "restorative justice" in the criminal justice field) is composed of both prevention strategies and behavior response strategies. For the purpose of this reading, "restorative practices" will be used to describe the proactive component of building relationships and developing community, while "restorative justice" will be used to describe the behavior response strategies, such as repairing harm and rebuilding relationships.

Restorative practices are based on the belief that when people feel included in a supportive community, they respect others in that community and become accountable to it. The key components needed to embed restorative practices are tolerance, respect, and supports that lead to belonging and acceptance. In a school community, teachers who implement restorative practices are trained to work with their students in a collaborative way, utilizing solution-focused strategies that promote supportive relationships and building trust. The goal is for students and staff members to actively engage in the process, creating a sense of ownership within the school community.

With a sense of belonging, students become more invested in the problem solving of their school. When school staff members are active participants in these practices, students find them more approachable, caring, and trustworthy. This proactive approach helps to create an environment and culture that can quickly identify problematic issues. When there is an established culture of trust and connection, disruptive and aggressive behavior can be addressed as a school community in a nonthreatening, nonjudgmental, and collaborative way.

Restorative justice emphasizes repairing damaged relationships, restoring a sense of well-being, and reestablishing the homeostasis of the community. However, as a response to behavior, it requires a policy and practices that are open to a different approach to justice—a method that emphasizes opportunity and restoration, not discipline.

One fundamental idea of restorative justice is that people are happier, more productive, more cooperative, and more likely to make positive changes when those in authority do things with them, rather than to them or for them (Wachtel, O'Connell, and Wachtel, 2010). A response that is purely discipline focused does not offer the opportunity for the restoration of relationships or conflict resolution, often resulting in a repeat of the problematic behavioral choices.

In response to misbehavior, one of the main goals in restorative justice is to help foster an understanding of how one's behavior affects others. As Costello, Wachtel, and Watchel describe in their book *The Restorative Practices Handbook* (2019), young people are often unaware of how their behavior affects others.

For this reason, one of the most powerful restorative justice strategies is offering the offending student the opportunity to hear directly from the victim. This allows those who have been harmed to describe the impact of the behavior and express their view about the type of actions that are necessary to repair the hurt and restore trust. Frequently, this strategy includes the families of both parties, offering a collaborative and solution-focused meeting that provides the opportunity for healing and closure.

Additionally, restorative justice can help alleviate the shame that is associated with misbehavior, allowing the student with problematic behavior to rejoin the community, knowing that he or she has made genuine efforts to repair the damage done to relationships. Restorative justice allows the acknowledgment of a person's worth, while at the same time rejecting the problematic behavior.

Why should restorative practices be an alternative to suspensions or expulsions? Brewster and Louallen (2016) report that, once suspended from school, students are twice as likely to be suspended again, with a trajectory of dropping out. Once students drop out and/or are expelled, they are three times more likely to be incarcerated.

In addition, May (2018) reports that, according to a UCLA Civil Rights Project study of ninth graders, even one suspension can triple the chance of incarceration and double the chance that a student will drop out. Thus, it seems evident that without the proper supports in place, students who are suspended or expelled face a higher chance of recidivism.

Another argument in support of restorative justice is that out-of-school suspensions contribute to an increase in unsupervised time. Suspending students removes them from an environment with structured school supervision, increasing their opportunities to become involved in problematic or criminal activity. This loss makes it more difficult for students to succeed academically and decreases their access to positive peer and adult relationships.

Also, suspensions and expulsions are often impersonal and devoid of closure, offering students little opportunity to learn how their behavior affected others. If a person who has harmed another does not have the opportunity to restore the relationship, he or she is likely to seek new relationships with others who have made similar problematic choices and end up alienated and marginalized.

Additionally, stigmatizing the students with problematic behavior by labeling them in a way that sustains their sense of shame and alienation often promotes and amplifies future problematic behavior. Watchel, O'Connell, and Watchel (2010) reiterate that many criminal justice systems and school disciplinary systems often fail to capitalize on the opportunity to redirect shame in a constructive way. Often our young people do care about relationships and will be better served when given the opportunity to restore them.

Therefore, when possible, restorative justice strategies can be used effectively as an alternative to suspensions or expulsions. (Obviously, there will be scenarios in which student behavior is at a level where suspension or expulsion is not negotiable. However, there are many instances in which students have been removed from school for behaviors that do not warrant such disciplinary measures.)

Some critics of restorative justice argue that victims should not be asked to participate in a meeting with the person who has harmed them, since the exposure might be uncomfortable or feel unsafe. However, Lyubansky (2019) notes that victims often request such dialogue to highlight the consequences and harm of the behavior.

Additionally, many victims desire a sense of closure, which is often the end result of restorative justice. Furthermore, restorative justice is not a forced strategy. Although the student who caused harm and the victim must agree to participate in the intervention, neither party is required to make a promise to apologize or forgive. The ultimate goal is to produce mutual agreements and understanding on how to move forward from the isolated incident.

Another criticism of restorative justice is that the process does not teach students accountability and does not offer realistic consequences for inappropriate behavior. However, when it is implemented with integrity, students learn accountability by being active participants in the process, restoring harmed relationships, acknowledging emotions, and seeing the impact of loss or damaged property. Following through with the agreements and resolutions is a more personal and accountable response to the behavior than paying a fine or participating in community service, both of which are disconnected from the emotional or psychological consequences of the incident.

Using restorative practices and restorative justice within the structure of preventive behavioral threat assessment and management is a key component to creating meaningful social connections and inclusion, which are two of the most important and effective violence prevention strategies. In the second section of this book, you will learn of seven unique and potentially violent student situations, along with the intervention strategies that address situations through the lens of restorative justice.

To increase equitable outcomes, combat bias, and restore relationships and trust, those who use threat assessment systems must understand that the focus is on facts and behavior unique to the situation rather than on profile characteristics, and that prevention, safety, inclusion, and connection are the desired outcomes of the management process.

TEST YOURSELF

1. To address potential ethnic and cultural inequities of service within a school district's behavioral threat assessment system:
   a. Focus on the demographic characteristics that are typical of active shooters.
   b. Find a normal explanation for what behaviors are being presented.
   c. Use an equity lens to assess the impact of your process on underrepresented or underserved populations.
2. When implementing the Salem-Keizer Cascade Model, use an equity lens to:
   a. Make sure the workload is distributed equally to everyone.
   b. Identify a lack of balance in the curriculum.
   c. Assess the impact of your process on underrepresented populations.
3. A strategy that can alleviate various forms of bias is:
   a. Encouraging team members to openly share their perspectives.
   b. Allowing school administrators to make threat assessment decisions independently.
   c. Looking for evidence to confirm preconceived notions.

4. When using restorative justice as an intervention strategy, remember that students:
   a. Respond most positively to punishment.
   b. Are often unaware of how their behavior affects others.
   c. Are not interested in restoring hurt relationships.

Answers: 1-c; 2-c; 3-a; 4-b

Chapter 3

Special Education and Preventive Behavioral Threat Assessment

One core element of behavioral threat assessment (BTA) is understanding whether a situation involves someone simply making a threat or actually posing a threat of extreme aggression. In student threat assessment, the majority of situations that teams encounter are found to be reactive in nature or indicate that a threat was made but not posed.

This is often true with students who have been identified as having disabilities who are receiving special education services. Because of this, BTA teams must have a solid understanding of disability and the practical and legal implications of special education and Individualized Education Programs (IEPs). This chapter will discuss the referral of students with disabilities for threat assessments, the interaction between threat assessment and special education processes, and how to steer clear of unintended problems during the initiation of the threat assessment process for students with disabilities.

Students who make threats or engage in mild to moderate aggression toward others often have lagging skills, frequently in the areas of communication, problem solving, emotional regulation, or social skills. They might be children who are impulsive or who have experienced significant trauma. This is true regardless of a student's chronological age.

Consider the behavior of young children. Because of limited communication and problem-solving skills, they occasionally use aggression or extreme language to express frustration, seek attention, or pursue their needs. When these lagging skills persist past a developmental age when the skills are typically acquired, despite consistent teaching and modeling, a disability might be present.

Federal special education law mandates that students who display indications of disabling conditions be evaluated to determine whether they meet criteria for special education and qualify to receive an IEP. Categories of disability include intellectual disability, communication disorder, visual impairment, hearing impairment, orthopedic impairment, learning disability, health impairment, traumatic brain injury, autism spectrum disorder, and emotional or behavioral disabilities.

Though we would not expect most of these conditions to result in a discrepant frequency of threatening or aggressive behavior when compared with the behavior of peers, several of these conditions might result in an increased frequency of threatening behavior due to the presence of the lagging skills previously mentioned.

Students with emotional or behavioral disorders, traumatic brain injuries, autism spectrum disorder, and health impairments such as ADHD are not necessarily more likely to engage in targeted aggression than their peers, but the characteristics of a disability can lead to increased frequency of reactive verbal or physical aggression. These students might engage in threatening or aggressive behavior that is more likely to come to the attention of others.

The challenge in the school setting is that threatening behavior, regardless of the education status of the student involved, must be addressed to maintain both the physical and psychological safety of everyone in the school environment. Therefore, students with disabilities may be referred for threat assessments, even when their disability could be a primary cause of the behavior.

The threat or behavior could be benign, or it could be a feature of impulsive or emotional communication, but the disruption to the school setting requires a response. In these situations, completing an efficient assessment, then encouraging the IEP team to address the behavior through long-term interventions, is a reasonable course of action.

In some cases, engaging in the threat assessment process alerts the team to suspected unidentified disabilities and necessitates consideration of an evaluation for special education. For instance, a pattern of reactive aggression displayed in response to certain triggers might indicate the presence of a disability. Though targeted aggression is not indicated in this case, engagement of the BTA leads to appropriate and necessary interventions. When targeted aggression is identified as a concern, the BTA process can serve the same function.

Consider a case that involves multiple situational factors that increase concern for targeted aggression, such as the presence of an identified target, motive, concrete planning, suicidal ideation, and hopelessness. A student in this situation might present with characteristics of an emotional or behavioral disorder and, in addition to other management strategies, could benefit greatly from a special education evaluation to clarify educational needs.

The Protecting America's Schools research from the United States Secret Service (2019) assessed completed incidents of targeted school violence from 2008 to 2017 and stated that "most attackers experienced psychological, behavioral, or developmental symptoms." Though this data set is a very small sample size, it is clear that students with these needs would benefit from efficient and effective interventions to mitigate harm to others or themselves as well as to increase coping skills, educational success, and life satisfaction.

Since students with disabilities will be referred for threat assessments, it is important to collect data to monitor and analyze these referrals. Data could include the frequency of assessments by education status (general education, special education, and Section 504), special education eligibility categories of the referred students, and whether the situation was targeted or reactive or did not pose a threat. Once these data are collected, considering asking these questions as a team:

- Are you seeing the pattern you would expect? Situations involving students with disabilities are more likely to be reactive than targeted.
- If overrepresentation of students with disabilities is present, is it specific to schools or programs, or is it occurring district-wide? If it is specific to schools or programs, are there additional supports or training needed in those settings?
- Are there specific eligibility categories overrepresented? If so, analyze why. Is there education or support needed for the staff members working with these students?
- Is there a discrepancy in the rates of exclusions, arrests, or other punitive measures for students with disabilities compared with those of students without disabilities?

It is critical that threat assessment teams strive to build a process that is equitable for students with disabilities. Including members with expertise in working with students with disabilities is a necessity. If a student of concern has a disability, ensure that the team includes a staff member experienced in working with students with that specific disability. Next, collect the data indicated above and analyze patterns with your team.

If you identify a concerning pattern, review individual cases to determine whether the referral or outcome was appropriate. If you find that particular schools or programs are referring students with disabilities more frequently than expected, consider if proactive supports might be needed. In programs with students with significant behavioral needs, you may consider referring for threat assessment only when targeted aggression is clearly present, as reactive behavior is likely a common occurrence.

When completing the threat assessment process for a student with an identified disability, be mindful of how the threat assessment and special education processes interact. Participants in threat assessment meetings need to understand that threat assessment meetings are not IEP meetings. They might have similar members, but they are used for different purposes.

If both a threat assessment and an IEP meeting are needed, be clear about when one meeting ends and the other begins, as IEP meetings have specific legal requirements, timelines, and permissions. Also, decisions made as part of the threat assessment can inform the IEP but cannot override decisions made by the IEP team. Examples of information gained in a threat assessment that can inform the special education process include:

- The concerning behavior identified: The IEP team might determine that the student needs an IEP goal or goals to address the behavior identified within the threat assessment and support the student.
- Triggers: Identified triggers for threats or aggression can inform a functional behavior assessment, the development of a behavior support plan, and the identification of needed accommodations.
- Protective factors (inhibitors): Understanding a student's strengths and interests is necessary for the IEP process as a whole but can also inform the functional behavior assessment or behavior support plan and identify accommodations that will most effectively support the student.
- The management plan: The plan can inform the IEP team on the services and placement that might be appropriate for the student. For instance, if a team notices that a student becomes extremely anxious around large groups of students and during transition times, the team might determine that the student would benefit from early arrival to school, late dismissal, or alternative passing periods to ease anxiety. This could affect placement, if the team determines that the student would benefit from taking fewer classes or briefly missing some class time.

The items above can be recommended by the threat assessment team, but they need to be agreed upon by the IEP team if they affect the IEP in any way. The bottom line is that students with disabilities will be referred for threat assessment, which is acceptable if the process is supportive, inclusive, focused on student needs, and not punitive.

Special education can be an incredibly supportive intervention for students by providing specially designed instruction in areas of need, accommodations and interventions, and connection with educators who are committed to students' educational and personal success.

TEST YOURSELF

1. Threat assessment teams need to understand which two of the following:
    a. The legal implications of special education.
    b. Characteristics of disabilities.

c. How to hold an IEP meeting.
d. How to use preventive BTA as a way to make a student eligible for special education services.
2. Which of the following is not an example of data to collect to monitor and analyze your system?
   a. The special education eligibility of students referred for threat assessment.
   b. Frequency of parent attendance at IEP meetings.
   c. Determination of reactive aggression, targeted aggression, or no posed threat.
   d. Frequency of threat assessment by education status.
3. Behavioral threat assessment can inform the team about:
   a. The discipline that would be most effective for the student.
   b. The staff member who should be working with the team on IEP goals.
   c. Whether a suspected disability might be present.
4. When creating a management plan, threat assessment teams should:
   a. Decide that the student's IEP is inappropriate.
   b. Revise the student's IEP in the threat assessment meeting.
   c. Be cautious of decisions that could affect the student's IEP.
   d. Attempt to determine a mental health or special education diagnosis that can explain aggressive behavior.

Answers: 1-a, b; 2-b, 3-c; 4-c

PART II

Meet the Students

Seven Potentially Violent Situations

Chapter 4

Daniel and Will

This chapter begins the introduction to the seven students and their unique situations to be examined in this book. Each case is genuine and has actually occurred; however, names, genders, ages, and other features of identity have been changed or combined with those of other cases to protect the individuals involved and to show that violent behavior is not limited to any one group, as stereotypes would have it.

In addition, several of these case studies exemplify particularly concerning situations that actually occurred, while others are more typical situations that school teams will encounter. Because of this, several of the case studies necessitated more extreme measures and creative solutions to protect the safety of those involved and to allow for the students to receive the support and intervention they needed to move their situations onto a more positive trajectory.

Let's begin with Daniel and Will, two high school juniors.

DANIEL

It's the end of the school day, and two boys, Daniel and Will, have started fist fighting by the lockers near the school's entrance. Daniel, the smaller of the two boys, is swinging wildly with his hands, throwing punches at and around Will. Will is in greater control of his fighting skills and is clearly winning.

The commotion has attracted a few other students and a couple of parents who are picking up their kids. Two teachers are also close to the fight and are heading over to break it up. A school administrator makes her way over to the boys first, and as she walks up, she hears Daniel scream, "One of these days I'm going to get my dad's shotgun and blow your motherfucking head off!" Will quietly, almost under his breath but audible to the administrator, says, "We'll see who has a gun . . . we'll see."

The school administrator and a teacher are able to stop the fight and separate the boys, then take them both to the office, where they are seated in separate spaces. As the administrator prepares an ice pack for Daniel to place on his swollen face, one of the parents and one of the teachers present at the fight follow the administrator and inform her of their fear about Daniel's threat. The parent states that he believes Daniel will become a school shooter and says he will post his opinion and describe the incident on social media if Daniel is allowed to remain at school. The teacher states that she will not return to work until Daniel is removed or arrested.

Daniel calms down and says that he is sorry for threatening Will and that he didn't mean it. He tells the administrator that he doesn't understand why Will hates him so much and that the resentment caused them both to lose their temper. He quietly states that he's been working on controlling his language and temper but that confrontation with other boys always gets the best of him. With a wry smile, he points to his swollen eye and reminds the administrator that he still has a ways to go.

Daniel's father is primarily Spanish-speaking, so a bilingual administrator calls him. Daniel's father says that he is disappointed that Daniel has behaved aggressively and that he'll do whatever he needs to do to support the school. He reports that he does not have a shotgun—or any gun, for that matter. He reminds the administrator that Daniel has a history of saying aggressive and even threatening things when he is emotional but adds that he has made behavioral progress over the past year as a result of seeing a therapist and the support provided by the school.

Daniel's father describes Daniel as Mexican-American, relays that they have a strong family support system, and states that their cultural heritage is very important to the family. He ends the call by committing to be at any meetings needed to address the incident and also promises that Daniel will be very well supervised after school at home and if he is suspended.

The administrator speaks to the school law enforcement liaison, and she checks her records, noting that there have been no criminal incidents or domestic disturbance calls involving Daniel or members of his household. She is aware of Daniel because of a few past fights but is otherwise not involved with him.

The administrator knows Daniel well. Daniel is not a marginalized student. In fact, he has a large group of friends and adults whom he relates to. With the exception of his attention deficit hyperactivity disorder, he does not appear to have psychological problems or vulnerabilities. His parents supervise his time at home and do not allow excessive screen time or the viewing of violent movies and first-person-shooter games. He has not shown an interest in cultural scripts that promote bravado or antisocial behavior to solve problems. He does not exhibit weapons fascination, he has not experienced loss or humiliation, and while he can be easily frustrated, he does not have a history of depression, suicidal behavior, or a lack of connection with adults or peers.

His school achievement is average, his relationship with his parents is reasonably positive, and he does not appear to have suffered trauma. The counselor confirms that Daniel has been willing to learn coping strategies and has been making efforts to improve his behavior as he ages.

Because the assessment process is collaborative, the administrator speaks with another member of the Level 1 team and discusses whether to schedule a Level 1 assessment. They decide that while Daniel's situation is not concerning from the initial examination, his threat has caused considerable fear with a parent and a teacher, potentially causing further disruption to the school milieu through social media and rumor.

As a means of double-checking risk factors, to explore further steps to help Daniel learn alternatives to fighting and making threats, to decrease the potential hysteria from parent communication chains, and to alleviate the anxiety of the teacher, the administrator decides to pursue a collaborative, preventive threat assessment. That assessment will occur in chapter 11.

WILL

The administrator speaks with Will. Will is a white student who has somewhat poor hygiene and displays a lack of emotional expression. He is calm but refuses to discuss the situation, stating only that he has always hated Daniel because Daniel has made him feel bad in the past. He also states that he does not feel bad about the fight and will gladly hurt Daniel again if Daniel gets near him.

The administrator calls Will's father, who says that Will is out of control at home and that he and his wife have even asked the police whether they can take him because they cannot control him. His father says that Will really hates Daniel and has talked about getting even with him because Daniel interfered with Will's relationship with a girl, which Will felt ended his only chance at having a girlfriend. Will's father dismisses the administrator's request to pick Will up, telling her to have Will walk home. He sarcastically tells her that if she suspends Will, his son will just enjoy the days off and spend hours playing violent video games.

The administrator checks with the school law enforcement liaison, and she checks her records. She reports that Will's home has had three domestic disturbance calls over the past two months, all involving parental emergency calls stating that Will was yelling and breaking furniture. On one occasion, Will's parents asked officers to remove Will from their home. The request was denied but noted in the report. The officer also reported that Will's father made a police report six months ago that his .38 handgun had been stolen from his car. The gun was not recovered by the police.

The administrator's concerns increase. Will has had a marked decrease in his attendance and is failing his classes. Only his music teacher has a relationship with him, and that relationship has become minimal. The administrator checks with Will's other teachers, who state that they almost never see him and that when they do, he is withdrawn and detached.

Will's creative writing teacher reports that while Will has rarely completed assignments, he did write a short story several months back that outlined a vindictive attack by a young man named Walter on his enemy David. The attack involved a technologically advanced and powerful sniper rifle that can shoot around corners and through windows, with Walter locating David sleeping in his bed and murdering him in his sleep.

The fictional act was justified by David's ongoing treachery and ruthless behavior and was well cloaked as a mini-superhero story. The teacher had been concerned but was happy that Will had completed an assignment and didn't want to scare him off by questioning the plot.

Will's school counselor has attempted to speak with him several times about his commitment to school, but Will has refused to meet. His parents have also been difficult to reach and rarely return calls.

When Will was a sophomore, the school social worker did a suicide risk assessment because of a veiled comment Will made about wanting to be dead, but Will would not participate. When the assessment was reported to Will's parents, they said they would address the issue and take him to a counselor, then reported back saying that the matter had been addressed. The counselor also reports that Will's family appears to struggle financially, and she believes that Will has been ashamed of his parents' ongoing challenges with unemployment and by not having a nice house, clothes, or school supplies.

Will rarely interacts with other students; however, he has been seen speaking with Dale, another junior and a student assistant in the office. The administrator calls Dale in and tells him that she is worried about his friend Will because he seems angry and uninterested in school. Dale tells her that he does not really consider Will to be a friend and that he does not want anything to do with the situation. She is puzzled by the extreme reaction and encourages Dale to say more. Dale appears tentative and uneasy. He avoids eye contact and says he is worried that Will will find out that he spoke to her and asks to be left alone.

She pushes further, and Dale hesitantly tells her that the fight might be the straw that breaks Will. He says that Will has bragged that he knows where Daniel lives and even which room he sleeps in. He says that Will knows that Daniel likes to hang out at the mall during the week. He says that Will has hated Daniel since the eighth grade because Daniel made a comment about

Will's haircut at the time—a well-quaffed mullet with a strand of blue coloring. Dale further stated that Will's animosity has grown because he thinks that Daniel stole his girlfriend and that Daniel's friends now tease and humiliate Will during passing time and after school. Dale reports that Will has said that if Daniel and his friends don't leave him alone, they will all get what's coming to them.

The administrator asks Dale whether Will has a gun, and he shakes his head but does not say anything. She presses further, and he asks whether Will will find out about this discussion. She promises that he will not, and Dale reports that Will brought a gun to school a few weeks back but that it was unloaded. He says Will told him he was just bringing it to see what it felt like to have a gun at school. Will also told Dale that he knows where Daniel lives and had taken the gun with him a few times as he walked past the house. Dale says he knew that he should have reported the gun but that he didn't believe anything would happen because it was not loaded.

The administrator searches Will's locker and finds a notebook with a list of names that match Will's friends and another statement that says, "I have everything I need to take out my enemies. I could outdo Columbine!" She also finds a drawing that appears to be of the school, with entries and exits identified along with time notations. The notations match the schedule when the doors automatically open for student traffic. Another notation is made identifying a location that could be the liaison officer's office. There is also a time listed that corresponds with the officer's lunch break.

The liaison officer interviews Will and pushes for information; however, Will refuses to speak with her, saying he doesn't really care what happens to him.

The administrator calls Will's father back to report what she's learned. He resists her request to check Will's room, stating that he and his wife "never go in there." She presses him to take a look, and he hesitantly agrees to check the search history on Will's computer. He finds several Google entries investigating the Columbine attack and other school shootings. There is also a Google Maps search for Daniel's address, including links to the Street View. There are also a Google Maps search and some saved screenshots of the mall from both the street and aerial views.

She asks Will's father whether Will could have stolen the gun, and he responds sadly, "With all of this crap I've just learned, probably so. This is very disheartening to me. My son was once a kind and caring kid who loved to play the guitar, sing, and do his schoolwork."

The liaison officer asks Will about the gun, and Will admits that he has it in his room and says that he might have brought it to school to show friends but denies that he intends to use it on Daniel. He says that his drawing, his journal, and his short story are all just fantasy fiction because he has been angry and bored. He says, "Writing and drawing violent stuff makes me feel better."

Will is arrested for both stealing the firearm and taking it to school. In Oregon, possession of a firearm by a juvenile at a school constitutes a mandatory arrest (ORS 419.C080 (3)). Will is transported to the juvenile detention center, where he will remain until his next hearing. Then he will likely be released to his parents' custody if a safety plan can be developed. Will is also suspended, pending expulsion (in Oregon, possession of a gun in school results in a mandatory expulsion).

Chapter 5

Alison

Alison, or Al as she prefers, is a 17-year-old student, two months from her 18th birthday. She is white, academically and intellectually gifted (IQ above 140 with a 4.0 GPA), and under tremendous pressure from her parents to be successful.

Her parents are very assertive about Al's academic success and college choice. They are controlling and insist that Al will attend their alma mater, a notable university in their hometown, regardless of Al's desire to explore other universities. While Al is quick witted and extraordinarily driven to learn and study, she lacks the confidence to assert her goals over her parents' demands. As a result, she is extremely resentful of her parents' control.

Her parents were similarly controlling with Al's older sister, Nicole, who is also extremely intelligent and academically outstanding. To spite her parents, Nicole refused to attend college at all and moved to Florida, where she works as a barista. She and Al remain close. Al's parents are affluent, intimidating, and litigious. One is a professor at a university, and the other is an executive at a big tech company.

Al attends a public middle/high school through an interdistrict transfer about 15 miles from her hometown. The school has an advanced academic track that Al's parents pay tuition to access. She has been at the school since the sixth grade.

Teachers consider her to be a know-it-all, and they have grown tired of her frequent comments about facts and accuracy in the details of their instruction. Al is usually correct, though, being more intelligent and informed than most, if not all, of her teachers.

Students have teased Al for years, mostly because of her condescending attitude toward them, but also because she was caught with an iPod in the eighth grade that contained downloaded porn. She had attempted to share the porn with other students to win their friendship, but the gesture backfired, and they used it to humiliate her. Most students have forgotten the incident at this point, and teasing has lessened. In fact, according to teachers, students have stopped teasing Al entirely and just avoid her because she can be extremely intense.

Al holds grudges and perceives the social rejection among her peers as bullying. A year ago, another student, Maria, was running the track with Al during PE and thought it would be funny to wrestle her to the turf in a headlock and give her a head-noogie. It was intended as a playful gesture, but Al reported it as an attempted strangulation. Witness accounts, including the PE teacher's, did not support Al's perception; however, Al insisted that it was malicious. Although Maria apologized, Al continues to bring the incident up as an example of injustice.

Al has a 16-year-old female love interest, Alex, whose parents are against the relationship, they say because of an age discrepancy of almost two years.

Al and Alex have a secret email account that they use to communicate. The account contains an ongoing draft email that allows them to write messages back and forth to each other. By using the draft, they avoid transmitting any data between servers from either of their home or school accounts, thus remaining clandestine.

Two months ago, Al's parents took her computer away for reasons they did not disclose. Al brags that she uses her phone to access the secret email account and to communicate through text messages.

Early one morning, Alex's mother discovered the open email account on Alex's home computer and read an entry written by Al the previous night, which greatly concerned her. She called the school counselor to report her concern. The email entry read:

> Baby,
> I don't know just how quite to say this. So I will just say it. I need mental health. I have gone insane over the past year. I can't handle all this pressure anymore. Today's bullshit just highlights my pain. School continues to only get harder, so I have lost my reasoning to deal with it. Losing control of it has caused me to lose control of my life. Losing my computer has lost the one place where I could vent stress. Those assholes, Matt, John, Blake, Maria, and just about everywhere I go . . . or anything I do . . . I get made fun of. It's pushed the 17-year lock on the stress that I have bottled up in my mind. I can't take it anymore. I have contemplated many options, and I will take them in numbered order in the list I made last month. This time I'm serious. This is my last strand of reason in this world, for I have nothing left. I am literally bleeding right now. I have begun to hurt myself. I don't see any happiness in it, so that's off the list. I am in such pain no words can describe.

The school counselor and the assistant principal ask Alex to meet with them to discuss Al. They inform her that they are concerned about Al and request her help. At first, Alex resists. However, she eventually admits that

Al is becoming increasingly agitated and angry about four students—Matt, John, Blake, and Maria—who judged her and humiliated her often with simple looks or smirks. Alex shows them a note that Al had written a few weeks ago. It reads:

> *I have a list of things I can do to keep my pride. But the last is a big, ugly thing because they may only understand drastic actions, and their perfect box is about to get fucking shot in the goddamn head with a pistol I can steal from my parents' bedroom—if my list reaches the last number. I love you with all my heart, and with my last days of logic remaining, I will explain: I normally can control my rage and may be able to regain control by the end of the night. However, this is the longest and most furious rage I have ever lost reasoning over. I refuse to talk to my parents, they don't understand. I don't want medicine or drugs, I want blood. I want those four to die. I want death to own their souls, and the devil to torment them forever more. I love you baby and I can't imagine a better girlfriend, but I'm so tired of it all. The pistol is in the same spot that my parents hid it, but every night I practice sneaking it into my backpack. It's really easy, surprisingly. I will kill Matt, John, Blake, and Maria before I kill myself. If I reach the last option that is.*

Alex tells the counselor and the administrator that Al was still really upset about Maria's trying to "strangle" her and that Al refuses to talk to the school counselor or anyone else about it anymore. She quotes Al:

> *All the administration does is sit around and be politically correct. They don't do any real work to get the job done. The attack on me last year in track was never dealt with. Maria strangling me was dealt with by a half-assed apology that she did not even mean. I know she thinks she got away with it. And Matt and John just laughed and encouraged her. Teachers, administrators, counselors don't do shit!*

The counselor and the administrator ask Alex about the list. Alex says Al keeps it in her locker.

The administrator asks the counselor to stay with Alex and leaves to find Al. She assures Alex that Al will not be told that Alex had provided the information. Al is not in class, and no one in school knows where she is. The administrator calls Al's parents, who say they don't know where she is either. They try to call her, but she does not pick up. Al's parents demand to know what is happening and threaten to sue if the administrators do anything to harm Al's reputation or cause a scene. They become agitated, stating, "If you even think of kicking Al out of school, we'll sue you personally and sue the district. We pay tuition for our daughter to attend this school! Do you know who we are? You better learn!" They say that they will drive to school to find Al and that she had better not be in trouble.

The administrator and a campus security officer search Al's locker and find a journal. In the journal, Al has written the following:

> Option 1: *I will talk to Teressa (my friend, my mom's friend) she has a PhD and is a very successful psychologist. She of all people I think will understand my rage and could help me somehow.*
>
> Option 2: *If I can't get a hold of Teressa, I will try my sister. She is next in line. She understands me like no one else.*
>
> Option 3: *I will take the .22 pistol into school, wait till one of them pulls a smart comment or insults me, then stick the gun in their face. I will not harm anyone else but will show EVERYONE what happens when you BRAIN FUCK a kid who has done ABSOLUTELY FUCKING NOTHING to them, and they will take EVERYTHING from me, including my reason to live. So I will take their fucking life as revenge. Two bullets to the head for each of them.*
>
> *I keep trying to imagine a perfect life in New York, in my air-conditioned house with fast internet, a great relationship with my life partner, kids, a job, a college education, and a great computer. But it's just not going to happen. It's too far away. I can't escape my controlling parents or even get that far away. My parents keep telling me I have to go to their college, which of course is right next to my house practically. I can see why Nicole was so pissed off. They don't really want me to go to the college I want. It's always what they want. I see no further point in living. The only reason I keep getting up is because I think maybe today will be better. I can see my girlfriend and what few friends I have, but it's just not worth it anymore. I get hurt more and more each time I get up. I thought of just suicide, but then those assholes would move to another target. I must remove those diseased shit-bags from the world. Their families and asshole friends will all see what they drove me to and take note.*

The administrator and the security lead look through a notebook from Al's English class. On the back page, there is an entry dated the previous week. It reads:

> *The gun is loaded and in my mom's hidden compartment. There's extra ammo in the closet. Every day I practice taking it and putting it in my backpack. So easy, they don't even know. What idiots. I'm shaking as I write this because I'm SICK of this shit. Maria and her boytoys are going to get what they deserve, or they better leave me the fuck alone. If they don't, it's time to cleanse the world, in the name of God. The perfect music that drives my rage is the song "Animal I Have Become" by Three Days Grace. I can control myself now, but it may not last. By the end of this month, either I will regain my sanity or there will be blood, I swear it. My own mini-Columbine!!!!!*

The administrator calls the SRO, the remainder of the administrators, and school security, and they all immediately begin searching for Al. As they do, the counselor receives a report from several students that Al has posted a statement on Twitter that reads:

> I'm about at the end of my rope! You know who you are and what you've done. Be ready, because death is too good for you, and you can be found wherever you try to hide. School is no exception!

As the administrator is notified of Al's Twitter message, Al is spotted sitting on the lawn about 50 yards from the building. The SRO approaches her carefully and asks her if she can talk. Al seems surprised but does not resist. The administrator takes her backpack and holds it away from Al. They are joined by the city's mobile crisis response team, which pairs a law enforcement officer with a mental health specialist who assists with a full search of Al and her belongings and conducts an interview with Al. Al refuses to speak to them initially, then says she stands by everything she has said. The backpack does not contain a weapon.

The mobile crisis response team determines that they have probable cause for a peace officer hold, as they believe there is imminent concern that Al is a danger to herself and others. They also make a referral to the juvenile department on a disorderly conduct charge because of the tweet she posted and the fear it caused among other students. Al is transported to the local mental health crisis facility. Al's parents call a lawyer and inform the school administrator that they will be suing the district for humiliating her in front of the student body and to mandate that she be allowed to return to school immediately.

At the crisis facility, Al meets the mental health professional, who is also a member of the Level 2 threat assessment team. Al breaks down, admitting that she felt like she was out of control and wanted to kill the four students. She says the whole thing is humiliating and embarrassing. She insists, though, that she was going to try to speak with her mother's friend, Teressa, or her sister, but if that didn't calm her down, she was willing to die to get rid of those who torment her and other students. She states that she just wants it all to end and that she hates her parents. She wishes she could move out and attend another school with smarter people and finish classes to get her diploma.

Al's parents refuse to cooperate with the mental health evaluator and juvenile department, deny having a gun, and will not turn Al's computer over to the police.

The juvenile district attorney, who is also a member of the threat assessment team, calls the threat assessment lead because Al's parents have called her and threatened their own legal action if charges are filed. The threat assessment lead outlines the safety concerns for the DA, who then contacts the parents to assure them that the team wants what is best for Al and also wants to keep others safe.

The school administrator informs the parents that a preventive behavioral threat assessment will be initiated and that interference with the resulting safety plan could be a form of neglect. If this is the case, the school administrators and juvenile department case workers have an obligation as mandatory reporters to inform protective services. The parents confer with their attorney, who advises them to cooperate in exchange for Al's eventual release.

To avoid the embarrassment of child welfare involvement and to assure Al's release, the parents admit to having the gun hidden in a safety panel under the bed and allow the police to take it and hold it at the precinct. The parents also allow the police to take Al's computer, which has multiple searches focused on school shootings, tactical operations, and instructions on using handguns. The parents stop cooperating at this point, refusing to discuss the situation further.

Chapter 6

Sam

Sam Smith is a 12-year-old white student in the fifth grade. He is a student with developmental delays and a communication disability, is on an IEP, and earlier in the school year was placed in a self-contained classroom for students with significant cognitive and adaptive needs. Since then, he has exhibited multiple instances of physical aggression and spoken threats toward staff members. He also has threatened to strike staff members with objects such as scissors and pencils.

Six injuries to staff members have been reported. The injuries have been of varying degrees, and some have necessitated medical evaluation and missed workdays. On March 15, Sam attempted to stab a female staff member with a pencil and yelled that he was going to kill her. A male staff member moved in between them and suffered a superficial wound from the pencil.

Sam has lived in a group home since early January and on multiple occasions has threatened to stab staff members with various items. He has also had four interactions with law enforcement when his behavior was beyond his mother's or the group home staff members' ability to maintain safety. He attempted to strangle his mother while she was at school enrolling him, and he has assaulted group home staff members repeatedly, sometimes causing injuries that required medical attention. A year ago, while living with his mother, Sam disassembled his bike and attacked his mother with the chain and a kickstand, causing a concussion and stitches.

Sam has made direct threats that match his acted-out behavior; however, he has not targeted a specific person. Sam's cognitive ability is limited, and there are no indications of research, plans, rehearsal, or attempts to acquire weapons. His thinking is not premeditative. His attacks are very dangerous and have been intended to cause severe harm, if not death; however, they are impulsive, and he utilizes found objects as weapons.

His targets are instructors in his classroom, specifically women between the ages of 25 and 40. He does not attack men, or women who appear older than 40.

Sam has superficial peer relationships, mostly due to his limited social skills and absence of insight. He has few skills to communicate his frustrations well and appears somewhat unaware of his offensive behavior. He does not have a history of trauma, and he does not appear to be experiencing depression or suicidal ideation. His relationships with his mother and the adults at the group home are strained due to his aggressive behavior.

His school achievement is commensurate with his academic functioning level, which is delayed and well below the normal range.

He has limited coping skills, which leads him to frustration and emotional escalation. He is extremely impulsive and frequently misinterprets basic social gestures as hostile. Sam is marginalized but somewhat unaware of that status. Sam prefers to be alone, looking at books and other material about dinosaurs, and is at his greatest comfort level when disengaged from other students or from staff members. He is heavily supervised at his group home and at school, and he is not allowed any time for gaming or watching inappropriate or violent movies or shows.

His psychological vulnerability creates a temperament that is easily triggered by any kind of confrontation or perceived attack. His supervision at the group home and at school keeps him from accessing weapons.

Because of the potential for others to be seriously injured during an aggressive episode, Sam's case manager asks for a preventive behavioral threat assessment and assistance with intervention and prevention ideas. The situation is referred to the school site Level 1 team.

Chapter 7

Eric and Maya

ERIC

Three female sophomores report that their friend Susan, a junior, has a boyfriend named Eric, who is also a junior. They say Eric brought a large knife to school and cut Susan on the hand while flipping it at her. They believe he intended to intimidate her because he thought Susan was going to break up with him. They report that they do not like Eric because he is very controlling of Susan, is always criticizing them, and continually tries to distance her from them.

Susan is called into the office, and she confirms that Eric did cut her on the hand; however, she believes that it occurred because he was showing off his knife-fighting skills, which he is very proud of. She also thought that maybe he was trying to intimidate her because she might be breaking up with him, but she was not sure. The administrator examines her hand and sees a superficial cut on the palm from when she raised her hand to block the knife. She does not believe Eric meant to cut her.

Susan confirms that Eric is controlling and monopolizes her time, but she insists that she really cares about him. She says that she is not worried about herself but that she believes Eric is likely to stab someone with his knife. She reports that he has been practicing his knife-fighting skills and intends to defend himself against four students who have tormented and bullied him since his freshman year. She says he is frequently humiliated and embarrassed by their harassment, causing him tremendous anger and resentment. She says he must walk home every day and cannot get to his house without passing the four students at their homes.

When asked about breaking up with Eric, she admits that she is considering it because of her concerns about his anger and potential violence toward other people, and she does not want to be a part of that. She says Eric dismisses her concerns and ignores her suggestion that he consider nonviolent solutions to his problems. She says that Eric thinks violent self-defense is his only option and that he accepts the consequences, which he thinks will give him street credit and a reputation as a vigilante.

The administrator calls Susan's mother to inform her about the event. Her mother very assertively asks to speak to Susan. Susan listens on the phone and assures her mother that she will do as she is told.

Susan hands the phone back to the administrator, and her mother says, "Eric did not intend to hurt my daughter. It was an accident. He was just showing off, and we want nothing to do with any of this from this point forward. Susan will not be speaking with you, the police, or anyone else about this. We will not be pressing charges or providing any other information. I'm coming to get my daughter and check out her hand."

Still holding the phone in hand, the administrator looks at Susan, who appears distressed and says, "I'm sorry this has caused a problem. Eric did not mean to hurt me. He was just messing around, and it was an accident. I do not want to talk about this anymore, and that includes with the police." She then turns her body away from the administrator, closing off conversation.

Susan's mother picks her up from school.

Eric is called into the office and found to be carrying a large lock-blade hunting knife. The knife is very sharp and sturdy. It is the type used to skin large animals. He matter-of-factly says he carries it to school every day and is more than happy to discuss why. He emphatically swears that he would never hurt Susan, that he loves her, and that someday he will marry her. He is proud that she is smart and wants to be a doctor. He says he carries the knife daily so he can defend himself against his enemies.

He boldly identifies his enemies as Kevin, Darren, Michael, and Jeff. Eric says these four boys have been bullying him since he started high school. He says they meet him after school on his path home and push him around, calling him derogatory names and humiliating him in front of his girlfriend. He says he is unable to get home without passing their houses.

Eric reminds the administrator that his mother cannot give him a ride because she is a "shut-in" and will not leave their home. Eric's mother was a victim of domestic violence by Eric's stepfather. Eric was a witness to the violence, which he reported during his freshman year. The report generated a visit from protective services and the police, which unfortunately escalated the situation, leading to an attack on Eric's mother by the stepfather that involved several hits from a baseball bat. Eric's stepfather is now in prison.

Eric reported that he found the knife in the woodshed and that it had belonged to his stepfather. He said that while his use of the knife has been limited to stabbing practice on a large punching bag in his garage, he is learning advanced knife-fighting skills from YouTube videos on the martial art Krav Maga, a fighting system used by the Israeli defense forces. Eric says that he is not ready to fight the four boys yet but that he believes he will be able to defend himself, using a knife, within the next three or four weeks.

He has been practicing his moves for about six months. He is insistent that he has a right to fight back with a knife, since there are four opponents and only one of him. As a longstanding victim of bullying, he believes wholeheartedly that he will become a hero for standing up for himself and says that nothing anyone says will convince him otherwise. He does not believe that an arrest will stick, since he is a victim, and thinks he is unlikely to be placed in jail. And if he is placed in jail for a while, it will earn him street credit.

The administrator attempts to convince Eric that his thinking is inaccurate, but Eric states that he does not believe it. He thinks the administrator and all school employees are weak because they were not able to stop the bullying when he reported it to his counselor as a freshman.

He politely, but assertively, tells the administrator that he is not interested in his help because he and society have already failed his mother and him. He says that he comes to school only because of Susan and that he intends to protect her, his mother, and himself for the rest of his life. He confidently states that he will not be a victim like his mother and that his mother supports his efforts to prepare to use a weapon if necessary.

The administrator asks Eric whether there is anything he can do to stop him from wanting to carry a weapon. Eric states that it is obvious but that he does not believe the administrator will be able to do it. He says the administrator must stop the bullying or he will eventually stab one, if not all, of the boys.

He says he knows that the administrator will take his knife but that he can get another one and will continue to find weapons as long as there are people in the world who would harm others just for fun or power. He says he knows he broke the school rules by carrying the knife but believes he has a right to defend himself and take control of the situation because that's what a real man would do.

Eric is a multiracial student (his mother is Asian-American, and his father is white) who is failing all his classes, is deficient in high school credits, is disconnected from teachers, and has only one friend, Susan. The school counselor reports that, while Eric was once an affable and academically engaged student, over the past two years, he has become uninterested in academics and unresponsive to efforts to help. The counselor is sad that the bullying has continued, because he believed that it had stopped during Eric's freshman year when he confronted the four boys and they promised they would leave Eric alone.

The SRO confirms that Eric was a witness to longstanding and considerable domestic violence directed at his mother by his now imprisoned stepfather. His mother is isolated, fearful, and hypervigilant, a condition she fosters in Eric.

The administrator calls Eric's mother, and she assures him that Eric would never hurt Susan, because he loves her and she is a light of hope in their world. She justifies Eric's right to carry a weapon and even says that at some point she would buy him a gun. She believes that he has been a victim but that the Krav Maga and the knife-fighting skills will make him a strong person so he does not end up like her.

She believes he has every right to defend himself against the four boys and fully supports his preemptive thinking. She also believes he will be a hero for standing up to the bullies, and she laughs when the administrator informs her that he will likely be arrested if this occurs. She tells the administrator that he is misinformed and that the police, social services, and the school leadership have never done anything to help her and her son and, in fact, have only made things worse.

She says that the public is sick of bullies and that she believes her son will be a real man if he stands up for himself. She describes Eric's suffering, his three years of depression, and suicidal ideation that resulted from the failure of society to protect them and insists that Eric is becoming a strong, confident young man. She is proud of him. The administrator asks whether there is anything he can do to help her, and she declines the offer, again stating that he has already failed her.

She reports that her fear and injuries have created a situation of considerable weakness and that she views herself as incapable of functioning in a normal life. She ends the conversation by suggesting that the administrator do something about those bullies or one of them will end up badly cut. She also says that, even if the bullies stop, Eric will continue to carry weapons so that he can protect himself and those he loves in the future.

Eric is undiagnosed but appears to have been experiencing depression, anxiety, and suicidality over the previous three years.

Eric is disconnected and has no identifiable positive relationships with prosocial adults in the community or school. He has no family members or even distant relatives involved in his life. His mother appears highly traumatized and struggling to survive. The two support each other's hypervigilance and are entrenched in an "us versus them" pattern of thinking. Their paranoia is clear; however, the bullying does appear to be a real issue.

Eric states that he knows he will likely be expelled for having the knife but says he does not care. He says that he hates school anyway and that he will wait for Susan every day after school and continue his relationship with her as they mature into adults. He says that he will not attend the alternative education high school or meet with a tutor because he knows he is going to fail school anyway. He notes that he cares for his mother, does the shopping, and should be able to get a good job. He also says that he has not done anything illegal and that he is simply saying he will defend himself if people continue to hurt him. And he again points out that there are four bullies and one of him, justifying the use of a knife.

The administrator asks Eric whether he will stop carrying the knife and attend the alternative high school for at least five days if school staff members can stop the bullying and get apology letters from the four boys. Eric pauses to consider, then laughs and says, "Sure, if you think you really can. But I will always carry a weapon, at least off campus, because there are more bullies and terrible people out there. Just ask my mother."

When the administrator investigates the bullying, he finds that Kevin, Darren, Michael, and Jeff are seniors and actually good students who are considered caring and kind by others. His investigation determines that while they have matured, they have continued to practice an immature pattern of bullying behavior with Eric after school, believing it was not really harming him.

When the four boys' parents are notified of potential violence and their sons' behavior, all of the parents are extremely upset, especially when they find out about how the bullying has hurt Eric. The boys commit to stopping the harassment immediately and write apologies. The administrator also asks their parents to write a group apology to Eric and his mother. They agree, stating their regrets and acknowledging their sadness about the domestic violence that Eric and his mother have suffered, something that was well known within the neighborhood. The bullying stops, and the apology letters are delivered.

The school administrator is concerned about safety but also concerned about the potential repercussions if Eric is expelled. He asks the threat assessment team for assistance in determining what to do next.

Eric, in an effort to lessen the attention on him, reports that another student, Maya, has shown her friends and several other students several knives earlier that day.

MAYA

Maya is a white sophomore who is well known among the faculty for creativity and her fashionable adaptations of vintage clothing into semi-medieval daily wear. She is brought into the office and found to be in possession of eight knives, varying in size and style. Most are of the fantasy or heroic-type design, with considerable ornamental and embroidered features. None are sharp or appear to be of a professional quality that would be typical of a weapon.

Maya reports bringing the knives to show at school because her friends are all very interested in weaponry, especially the type that accompanies fantasy games such as Dungeons & Dragons and Magic. She says she is in a fantasy game club with six peers. One of their hobbies is to collect ornamental knives and swords as symbols of power. She says she wishes she could find a dragon to accompany her weaponry because her power would increase even further.

She reports that she knows bringing the knives to school was wrong but that she could not resist because she had purchased them over the weekend at a flea market and was eager to show her friends. She apologizes and begs the administrator not to call her father because he will be very disappointed in her, as she promised him she would not take any knives or swords to school. The administrator informs Maya that he will have to discuss the situation with her father.

Maya and her friends are viewed by the school staff as average students who are somewhat immature and often involved in game playing. They enjoy each other's company, respond well to direction, and are generally well liked by teachers. Two teachers speak up for Maya, reporting that they have a great relationship with her. They state that they enjoy her creativity and slightly odd sense of humor. Her drama teacher has cast her as Seymour in the musical *Little Shop of Horrors*. Her band teacher says that her energy is excellent but that her trombone skills leave a lot to be desired. Still, she is always enthusiastic and enjoys playing music.

Maya has a history of impulsive and oppositional behavior as well as poor academics when she was in middle school. Her mother abandoned her father and her, becoming involved in drugs, and eventually became completely estranged from the entire family. Maya began experiencing depression and suicidal ideation as a result, losing interest in friends and academics. Her father made considerable efforts to help build their lives back, including counseling and frequent meetings with teachers and the school counselor. The efforts resulted in Maya's having successful freshman and sophomore years.

Maya's father is disappointed that Maya took the knives to school but blames himself for not realizing her excitement about the weekend purchase. He says that he will do whatever he needs to do to help the school employees and students feel safe but that he is concerned about the possible repercussions of school discipline. He is very cooperative with the investigation but worries about how Maya will respond if she is suspended or expelled and loses access to her friends, her school musical, and the positive school environment. He says that Maya is still in counseling and that her therapist considers her fragile, especially when dealing with loss.

Teachers consider Maya's father to be caring and attentive and doing his best with limited resources. They believe he will welcome support. The school counselor confirms that Maya's father monitors her educational progress and social connections and that he stays in contact with teachers.

Maya's father agrees to search her room, her computer, and her other belongings but does not find any indication of aggressive thinking or a motive to harm anyone. He says that while Maya is not necessarily popular, she is well liked within her social group and that she never speaks of enemies, social distress, or anger directed at others. Furthermore, her suicidal ideation that occurred two years earlier has been resolved, and she continues to receive considerable support from her friends and their parents, extended family, her therapist, and him.

When asked about thoughts or intentions of hurting herself or others with the knives, Maya becomes embarrassed and troubled about the administrator's perception that she might bring a weapon to school to hurt herself or someone else. She insists that she would never do such a thing and has no intention of giving the knives to someone who would. She says she only wanted to share them with her friends. She tearfully states that she is very sorry and wishes she had listened to her father.

Further investigation does not uncover any information suggesting attack motive, ideation, or preparation with Maya or her friends. In fact, further investigation confirms that Maya and her friends are fascinated by knives and swords as part of their role-playing games but are not using them or planning to use them as weapons against each other or other students.

Though Maya brought multiple knives to school, which is a clear violation of school policy, the administrator determines that suspension or expulsion would not be appropriate because her intent was not to harm or intimidate anyone. Furthermore, an expulsion would remove many protective factors, such as her role in the school play, her place in the orchestra, her positive connections with teachers and students, and her academic momentum.

Because Maya's possession of the knives at school led to rumors and exaggeration, the administrator determines that engaging the threat assessment process would be helpful to quell the concerns that are being shared. The administrator would also like assistance from the threat assessment team on determining restorative strategies that might be appropriate in this situation.

Chapter 8

Alan

Alan is an eighth grader who identifies as Hispanic and attends a large middle school. His parents are divorced. He lives with his mother and visits his father routinely on alternate weekends and Wednesdays. Yesterday evening, he communicated with another student, Carlos, on Facebook Messenger, and in that exchange, he stated that he was looking for someone to bomb the lockers of the jocks or shoot up the school for him. He provided links to websites on making bombs. He also stated that he was a psychopath and was looking for others to help who were just as crazy.

A school resource officer was called in to investigate the threat that evening. When asked, Alan said he was joking and just wanted to scare the other student. He said he had been researching bombs and watching videos of people being killed. The SRO searched Alan's phone and confirmed that Alan had indeed visited those websites. Alan stated that he watched the videos in order to desensitize himself and to be prepared for an upcoming apocalypse.

Alan insists he is not angry with anyone but says Carlos has had a grudge against him for a long time. He notes that he is willing to apologize to Carlos about the joke on Facebook, and he reports that he mentioned jocks as a target because he resents his own lack of skill at sports and the arrogant way the jocks behave. Alan states that his resentment is not powerful enough to motivate him to harm anyone and that he believes the only justifiable reason for violence is self-defense.

Alan says he understands that people need to take these kinds of threats seriously and that talking about school violence is scary because of events like Columbine. Furthermore, he notes that a friend had asked him whether he wanted to reenact Columbine last year and he thought his friend was "half joking." Alan is reluctant to give his friend's name but eventually reports that the friend is named Chris.

Alan's mother reports that she thought Alan was trying to get a reaction from Carlos and to anger him. She says she believed Alan wanted to play a mind game and manipulate Carlos into being out of control. She also reports that Alan feels disconnected from reality when he is online and that he would never say any of those things to Carlos' face.

The SRO confirms that the social media threats were written during an interaction with Carlos, who is also a student at the same middle school. The interaction appears to have been an act of one-upmanship that escalated to the hostile and threatening statements. The threats were specific and detailed, not only to the student population in general but also to the student athletes. While Alan claims that he was only joking in attempting to recruit someone to act out these violent intentions and that he just wanted to provoke Carlos, the school administration and threat assessment team are concerned about the potential for future violent ideation that might become more serious.

Approximately a year ago, Alan acted out aggressively when roughhousing with another student in a classroom and swung his musical instrument, accidentally hitting a teacher in the head and causing her a concussion. The incident was addressed through discipline, and Alan was remorseful. From that point on, he made positive gains with his behavior.

One year ago, a suicide risk assessment was conducted because Alan had stated that he was depressed and wanted to die or be killed. The assessment noted that Alan stopped having such thoughts after he underwent private therapy. The suicide risk assessment also specifically described two considerable sources of anxiety for Alan: his ambition as a musician (wanting to be the best) and his relationship with his grandmother.

Alan's mother confirms his tense relationship with his grandmother but says she works late and needs the grandmother to cook for and supervise her kids. She sadly reports that Alan feels considerable tension, with flashbacks and bad memories involving emotional abuse by his grandmother. She says he is very tense around his grandmother and has to think in the third person in order to cope with the stress.

In fact, according to Alan's mother, his resentment toward his grandmother led him to have thoughts of harming her or killing her. He even wrote an email to his therapist, describing his anxiety and how his grandmother caused him to become detached and uncaring and led him into a state of delusional thinking, including specific thoughts of how he would kill her. His mother says that she thought the intense feelings of anger had decreased through the private counseling sessions but that she is still concerned. She says she would be willing to return Alan to counseling to address his anxiety, his anger, and his relationship with his grandmother.

Further review of records confirms that Alan uses bravado and intimidation when he feels powerless but that he justifies aggression only as a self-defense tactic. He has a history of emotional dysregulation but is able and willing to take accountability for his actions and responds well to direction, although he is short on empathy and remorse.

Alan was previously referred for a psychoeducational evaluation for autism spectrum disorder and his ADHD diagnosis. However, his parents did not agree to the evaluation and withdrew him from school for the remainder of that year, claiming that his problems were a result of their divorce and saying that they would handle the issues with a private therapist. They re-enrolled him the following year.

Alan has had five disciplinary referrals—three for insubordination, one for sexually harassing language, and one for the aggression that caused the teacher's injury. The discipline records indicate that the insubordination and the sexually harassing language were within the scope of typical adolescent behavior. Furthermore, Alan responded positively to the disciplinary consequences and improved his behavior.

Alan's mother reports that she does not keep weapons in her house. His father, however, has guns stored in a safe, and Alan and his father frequently go target shooting. Alan also has his own BB gun and a place to fire it at his father's house.

Alan's mother deleted his Facebook and Instagram accounts after the SRO visit. However, through an open-source investigation, his posts previous to the threats were examined and found to be benign.

Alan's teachers report that they like him and enjoy his participation in class. They say that he is positive, friendly, and sometimes entertaining, even to the point of occasional disruption, and that his sense of humor is a bit dark and awkward at times, which has caused some peers to be hesitant in their relationship with him. Most of the time, he keeps the rules, is engaged in positive school activities, follows instruction, and makes a good effort to complete his schoolwork.

Alan likes his teachers and respects their opinions and authority. He willingly discusses his anxiety about improving his musical skills and openly shares that he wishes he had more time with his mother, who works long hours as an accountant and is rarely available. He also confirms that he is still very angry at his grandmother and would rather that she not visit his house or care for him and his siblings.

Alan has many protective factors, including music, choir, church, youth group, and his relationships with his father and his teachers. Alan reports that he is looking forward to attending college, becoming a lifeguard, and pursuing a music career. He reports that he wants to be in a helping profession, perhaps working as a school psychologist or school counselor. He states that he is assertive and confident, believes in himself, and is a moral and good person.

Alan has a girlfriend named Maria and one good friend named Eric. His other friendships are more superficial, although he greatly enjoys his interactions at his church's youth group. Maria is a year younger than he is and attends classes in a special education classroom for students with developmental disabilities. The school administrator confirms that both sets of parents do not allow Alan and Maria to be alone at this point in their relationship. Additionally, Alan is friends with a group of fringy musicians who listen to violently themed music.

Alan states that he plays violent video games, reads violent literature, listens to violently themed music, and watches zombie apocalypse videos because he wants to desensitize himself to death and enjoys the feeling of a fight-or-flight response. (Themes include targeted violence, basic shooter scenarios, and images of death.) He does not, however, act aggressively at home or talk about violence toward other people. Alan appears to have immersed himself in this type of entertainment, and his level of viewing is considered extreme at this point.

The school's threat assessment team constructs a safety plan for the days following the initial social media threat and schedules a preventive behavioral threat assessment that includes teachers, parents, and Alan's youth group leader (by parent permission).

PART III
Begin the Level 1 Process

Chapter 9

School Site Level 1

Preventive Assessment and Intervention

QUESTIONS 1:11 AS THEY APPLY TO THE SEVEN STUDENT CASE STUDIES

Now that the seven students and their concerning circumstances have been introduced, the book will turn to the process of assessing the cases for the presence of risk factors, protective factors, and prevention-minded management strategies. This chapter will introduce the first eleven questions in the Level 1 protocol. They are supported by multiple research studies, data sets, and the recommendations of experts in the field of behavioral threat assessment and violence prevention.

These sources are available in chapter 3, Supportive Research and Recommendation, of *Assessing Student Threats: Implementing the Salem-Keizer System, Second Edition* (Van Dreal et al., 2017). Additionally, the references and resources section at the end of this book contains many contacts that support that research as well as services and consultation that assist with preventive behavioral threat assessment.

The complete Level 1 protocol, which is a how-to guide that contains all of the instruction and material necessary for a multidisciplinary, school-site-based preventive behavioral threat assessment, can be found through a link in the appendix. (Note: In Daniel's case, the team assessment should include the teacher who was so concerned with Daniel's threat that he refused to return to work until Daniel was removed from school. The team approach and assessment questions will help differentiate the real concerns from the assumptions.)

After each question is presented, this chapter will discuss each of the seven situations identified in the preceding chapters and address the questions as they were answered by their respective threat assessment teams. The objective is to provide you with a thorough understanding of each assessment question and examples of how a threat assessment team might analyze each situation in order to identify risk and protective factors. Later chapters will address the interventions recommended in each of these cases, based upon each team's appraisal of each situation.

SITE-BASED LEVEL 1 QUESTIONS 1–11

Question 1

Note the severity of the threatened aggression on the continuum (see figure 9.1 below).

Does the communication or situation suggest a threat of low to moderate aggression, such as punching or fighting? Or does the communication or situation suggest a threat of serious or lethal injury, such as a severe beating, shooting, stabbing, or bombing? (The behaviors listed within the continuum are examples and not necessarily locked into their positions. In other words, hitting can be a mild, moderate, or even extreme form of aggression, depending upon the intention or the outcome of harm.)

Note that there is a change within the continuum from low to moderate aggression (nonsevere or nonlethal injury) to extreme aggression, or what is termed as violence (severe or lethal injury). Extreme aggression is also referred to as violence. If aggression was acted out, locate the outcome or intended outcome on the same continuum.

The intent of this question is to examine aggression as a continuum from mild to extreme, objectively assess the behavior that was threatened or suggested, and determine what was actually acted upon. Engaging in this examination can reduce panic and encourage a rational analysis of student behavior, which helps to increase psychological safety. This question is adapted from the work of the forensic psychologist Eric Johnson (Johnson, 2000).

> Daniel: Daniel has yelled a threat to shoot Will with his father's shotgun. So the first part of the question indicates a threat of extreme aggression (shooting). The second part of the question addresses actual behavior or acted-out behavior. In this case, Daniel is acting out moderate aggression or fighting. Of course, he is losing and makes the threat as an intention to intimidate Will, but his behavior is fighting, and it does not match his threat.
>
> Fighting is not the same as getting a shotgun and trying to kill someone. So currently the two do not match. And remember, in behavioral threat assessment, the goal is to examine whether the behavior or the situational risk factors match the perceived threat.

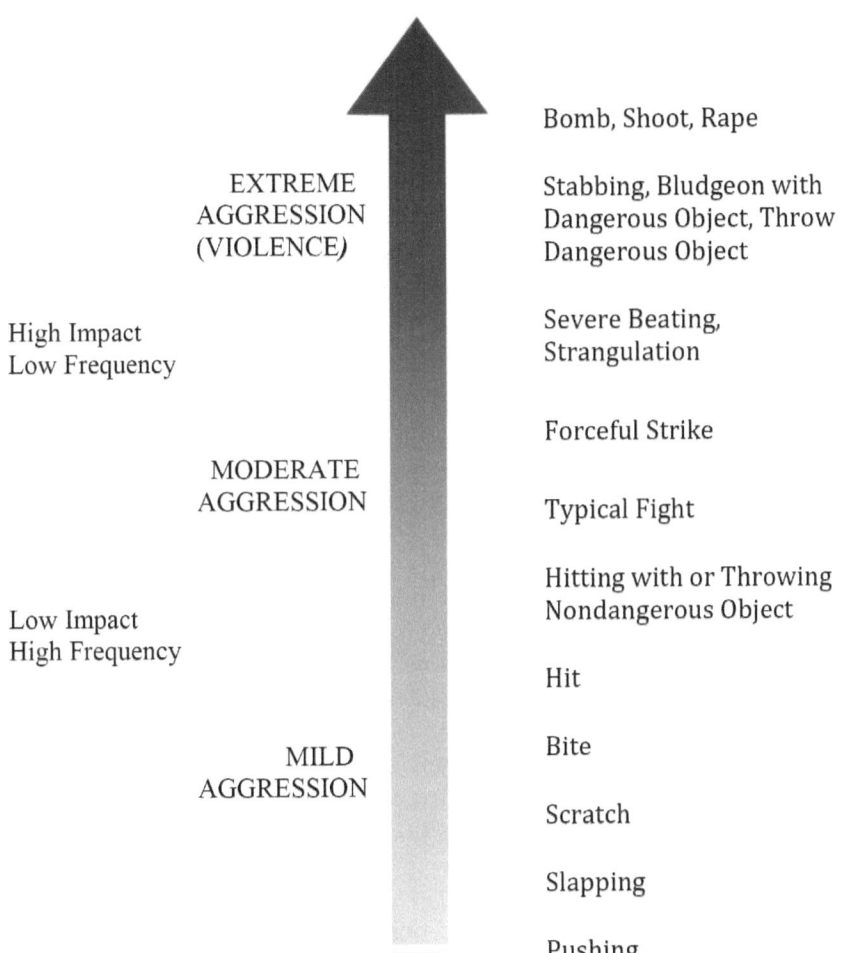

Figure 9.1.

Will: Will has also made multiple veiled threats of extreme aggression, to shoot Daniel. His acted-out behavior also includes fighting, or moderate aggression. Fighting is incongruent with acting out violently with a gun.

Alison: Al has made a threat to shoot four peers, so the threat is of extreme aggression. We have no knowledge of acted-out aggression, so the answer to the second part of the question is none.

Sam: Sam becomes impulsive, is easily agitated, and makes rageful aggressive, if not violent, threats, sometimes followed by aggressive behavior that can also have a violent outcome, such as stabbing someone with a pencil or attempting to strangle an instructional assistant. As the team considers his threats and his behavior, the answer to the first portion of the question is that Sam's threats are often of extreme aggression, to stab or strangle. His acted-out behavior is congruent with those threats, as he does attempt to strangle and stab others. So the second part of the question indicates extreme aggression as well.

Eric: Eric has communicated that he intends to stab the peers who are bullying him, so there is a threat of extreme aggression. The team is uncertain whether he intended to cut his girlfriend's hand with the knife but determine that his behavior toward her is moderately aggressive, nevertheless.

Maya: Maya has engaged in no threatening communications or acted-out aggression, so the answer to both parts of the questions is none.

Alan: Alan made communications regarding bombing the lockers of jocks or shooting up the school, both threats of extreme aggression. He has not engaged in any aggression regarding this situation, so the answer to the second part of the question is none.

Describe the details of the threat, dangerous situation, and/or acted-out behavior. Provide a short narrative objectively describing the incident.

In this question, teams should provide factual, objective descriptions of the situation. Providing a thorough narrative summary will assist your team in examining the situation as a whole, prior to assessing specific situational factors. The answers below provide examples of how responses to this question might be stated. The statements below contain the names of other students involved. You might wish to discuss the inclusion of the names of targeted students with your legal counsel.

Also, remember that accompanying documentation, such as journal entries, assignments, social media communications, etc., can be attached to the Level 1 protocol to provide further documentation, but references to such material also should be included in the team's answers to these questions.

Daniel: Daniel was in a fight with another student. While losing the fight, he made threats to get his dad's shotgun and shoot the other student. After the fight, Daniel de-escalated quickly, apologized, and noted that he had no intention to follow through on his threats. This is a typical behavior of Daniel. He is impulsive, he has been in physical fights before, and his parents and his counselor are working with him to teach him better coping skills. Furthermore, his parents deny that he has access to a firearm and supervise him at home. They have not identified any kinds of variables that would be consistent with Daniel's carrying out the threat he made.

Will: Will was in a fight with another student, and both students made reference to a gun. After the fight, Will stated that he hates the other student because he stole his girlfriend, and he threatened to hurt the other student in the future if he gets near him. Police have responded to the home twice in the past month because Will allegedly was yelling and breaking furniture. A peer reported that Will told him he knows where the other student lives and where he spends time.

The peer also reported that Will has brought an unloaded gun to school and had it while walking past the other student's home. Will has written in a journal about outdoing Columbine and listed the names of several of the other student's friends. In addition, Will appears to be making note of times and dates related to the accessibility of doors and offices in the school and has been researching the Columbine attack.

Alison: While in communication with another student, Al stated that she intends to kill four students because of ongoing bullying and harassment. She expressed feelings of rage and has multiple significant stressors. She stated that she has access to a firearm at home and has practiced putting it into her backpack.

Al referenced having two other options but said that if they don't work, she will take the gun to school and shoot each of the students, then herself. She then posted a comment online about being at the end of her rope and finding the people who are trying to hide, even at school. Al was located at school and did not have a weapon but was transported to the hospital for evaluation.

Sam: Sam is a student with disabilities that cause challenges with behavior and impulse control. He has become extremely aggressive to the point of severely harming school and group home staff members, as well as his mother. He has punched, stabbed with a pencil, and strangled others when emotionally escalated. His behavior does not appear to be planned or rehearsed, and his motives are uncertain. However, he does require considerable resources for behavioral management and safety planning.

Eric: Eric carries a knife daily so he can defend himself from his perceived enemies, who are four students at his school. Eric says the boys have been bullying him since he was a freshman. He says they meet him after school on his path home and push him around, calling him derogatory names and humiliating him in front of his girlfriend. He says he is unable to get home without passing their houses. He has been practicing knife-fighting skills using a system called Krav Maga and believes he will be proficient at fighting in two to three weeks. He insists that he will stab one or more of the boys if they continue to harass him, and he believes he will be seen as a hero and a vigilante in the public eye.

His mother supports his plan and refuses intervention. Eric will not back off of his plan and intention to use a weapon. Additionally, he might have used the knife to intimidate his girlfriend into staying with him. The gesture resulted in a cut to her hand when she attempted to block the knife. Eric denies that the injury was intentional and insists that he was only showing off, not trying to intimidate his girlfriend.

Maya: Maya brought eight knives to school to show her friends (six peers plus fifteen other students in the vicinity). The knives are ceremonial and of poor quality and represent part of a power structure related to several fantasy games that Maya and her friends play routinely. Maya denies any intent to harm herself or others. Investigation confirms that Maya was simply showing off her new knives and that there was no risk or threat associated with her behavior.

Alan: Alan communicated with another student over Facebook Messenger. In that exchange, he stated that he was looking for someone to bomb the lockers of the jocks or shoot up the school for him and provided links to websites on making bombs. He also stated that he was a psychopath and was looking for help from others who were just as crazy.

The SRO investigated, and Alan said he was joking and only wanted to scare the other student. He said he had been researching bombs and watching videos of people being killed. The SRO searched his phone, and this was confirmed. Alan stated that he watches the violent videos to desensitize himself so he will be ready for an apocalypse.

Question 2

Have there been communications suggesting a potential attack or act of aggression (i.e., direct threats, specific references, veiled threats, or vague warnings)?

Threats can be direct, through oral communication, art, email, social media, written language exercises, and other modes of communication. Threats can be indirect (e.g., ominous warnings) or veiled, even casual references to possible harmful events or previously occurring violent events (e.g., school shootings). A threat does not have to be specifically stated to be of concern, nor does it have to be stated or implied within the school setting.

Daniel: Yes. He has made specific and direct threats to Will during a fight. The communications appear to have been an intention to intimidate Will and end the fight. Daniel has made no other communications regarding harming Will or planning any kind of violent attack.

Will: Yes. Will has indicated, through different forms of language and communication, veiled threats and references to attacks on Daniel and Daniel's friends. He has told another student, Dale, that he has everything he needs to attack and seek revenge on the people who have offended him and humiliated him.

Will has written a short story with a theme of vigilante justice conducted by someone named David against someone deserving named Walter. Drawings and lists regarding potential plans were found. And a notebook and his computer contained lists of students who have offended him, along with grievances. Those students are all friends of Daniel, who has also been threatened directly and indirectly.

Alison: Yes. Through email, conversation, and social media posts, Al has expressed both direct and veiled threats, as well as ideation, motive, and plans to kill four students and herself at school. Her communications have been specific and detailed.

Sam: Yes. Sam typically communicates his intentions just before he attacks. All of his communications are very direct, emotional, and expressive.

Eric: Yes. Eric is very transparent about a plan to stab any of the students who have been bullying him. He has communicated it directly to his girlfriend, his mother, and the school administrator.

Maya: No. Maya has made no communications regarding aggression toward anyone.

Alan: Yes. Alan was involved in a conversation with a student on Facebook Messenger, where he appeared to be looking for someone to bomb lockers or shoot up the school. No other concerning communications have been reported.

Question 3

Are there indications of a plan, feasible process, or clear intention to harm others?

Threatening communication becomes more concerning with behavior that suggests intent to follow through with a targeted attack (called "pathway behavior" or "attack-related behavior"). Many threats are not stated directly but are indicated by vague references combined with behavior. Attack-related behavior might be, but is not limited to, the following:

- *A plan (complex or simple) to carry out a targeted act of violence against a specific individual, group, or student body. The plan would have a sequence of actions necessary for its success and almost always requires a motive. The more plausible and detailed the plan, the greater the risk.*
- *Acquisition of a weapon, attempted acquisition of a weapon, past possession of prohibited items at school, or research about how to acquire a weapon.*
- *Rehearsal (practice and simulation) of the plan or a similar plan. Rehearsal or simulation is often necessary before a targeted event can be completely planned and carried out. Rehearsal can be indicated through art, fantasy games, writing or film projects, the use of movies or internet sites with themes and sequences of targeted violence, first-person-shooter video games, etc. However, participating in such activities does not lead students to act out violently. Use of such materials is considered attack-related behavior only when used as rehearsal.*

- *Scheduling an attack. A scheduled attack may be clear and detailed or flexible, awaiting a triggering event (e.g., teasing, rejection, or loss) that further justifies the violence as a solution.*

Daniel: No. Though Daniel made a threat during the fight, he apologized and denied any plans to harm Will. Daniel's parents report that they have searched his room and his computer and have found no indications of plans or intentions to seriously injure or kill Will. In fact, they report that Daniel actually likes Will and is seeking his attention.

Through discussions with teachers, Daniel is described as an impulsive student who has been in physical fights, likely due to verbal behavior that irritates others. There have been no indications through his communications or his behavior that he is trying to acquire weapons or make a plan to harm Will any further than the fight.

Will: Yes. Will has engaged in multiple attack-related behaviors. He has schematic drawings of the school that would suggest he knows when the school doors open automatically and when the SRO is in her office. He has referenced a plan in his discussions with Dale and has written a short story that appears to be a played-out version of an attack on Daniel through his bedroom window.

Although the short story is somewhat fantastical, it still suggests that Will's ideation might be more than just fantasy. Investigations of Will's computer and phone identify Google Maps searches for Daniel's house and the mall where Daniel and his friends hang out during the evenings. Will has several schematics or drawings that would indicate he is assessing the school, the bell schedules, when doors are open, and when the SRO is in the building.

Will has also investigated previous school attacks, suggesting that he might be identifying the best means by which to conduct an attack himself. Will stole a .38 handgun from his father, took it to school, and had it in his possession while walking past Daniel's home.

Will's short story, his journal entries, his lists and maps, and his investigation on the internet all suggest that he has rehearsed and possibly even simulated the act of attacking Daniel and his friends. It does not appear, however, that there is a date noted. However, Will appears to be engaging in significant attack-related behaviors, so when it comes to scheduling, it might be that Will is awaiting a trigger, which might have occurred recently with this fight, suggesting that there is considerable urgency to this matter.

Alison: Yes. Al has communicated that she has several options to solve her problems with four students, but if she is unsuccessful in getting help, she has a concrete plan to wait until one of them insults her at school, then will shoot each of them twice in the head. Her plan ends in her suicide. She indicates that she has access to her parents' gun and has been engaging in rehearsal, in which she practices taking the gun from the place where it is hidden and sneaking it into her backpack. She also has access to ammunition. In terms of scheduling,

Al references the end of the month as a time when she will make a choice of whether she engages in her plan.

Sam: No. Sam has made direct and expressive threats that match his acted-out behavior. However, he has not engaged in targeting directed to a specific person. There are no indications of research, plans, rehearsals, or attempts to acquire a weapon. His thinking is not premeditated. His attacks are dangerous and intended to severely harm his victims; however, they are impulsively driven, and he utilizes found objects as weapons.

Eric: Yes. Eric has rehearsed and practiced his plan, which is to use a knife to cut and stab any of the four boys he sees as his enemies. He will do this when he thinks he has the expertise to be successful, which he states is approximately two to three weeks from now. Eric has done research on knife fighting, has a weapon, and claims he will find other knives if the school takes his away.

Maya: No. There is no indication that Maya is engaging in any planning, preparation, rehearsal, or scheduling related to aggression.

Alan: Yes. Alan has completed research on bomb making and violence. He communicated a plan regarding finding an accomplice to bomb the jocks' lockers or shoot up the school. While Alan denies that he intends to follow through and that his behavior was simply a joke, the team did not want to dismiss them as typical.

Question 4

Are there indications of suicidal ideation?

Is there a history of suicidal ideas, attempts, gestures, references, and/or intent? The wish to die, be killed, or die by suicide, combined with a threat to harm others, increases risk, especially if the self-destructive behavior is the last part of a plan to harm others and carry out revenge or justice.

Daniel: No. Through interviews with Daniel, his parents, and multiple school staff members, there are no reports or indications that Daniel is considering killing or harming himself.

Will: Yes. The school counselor noted that a suicide risk assessment was completed when Will was in the eighth grade. His father confirmed that Will had mentioned suicide when he was a middle school student and has said several times since that he wishes he were not alive or that someone would kill him. When Will was asked in an interview whether he had intentions to hurt himself or had thought about it, he refused to answer.

Alison: Yes. Al has communicated that the last part of her plan to kill others includes suicide. She stated that she has considered only suicide but decided she will kill others in addition as part of her plan.

Sam: No. There are no indications that Sam is thinking of killing or harming himself.

Eric: Not currently. He has a history of depression and suicidal ideation, but his confidence and self-esteem have improved as a result of his learning to fight.

Maya: Not currently. Historically, Maya has had difficulty coping with loss and experienced suicidal ideation because she was abandoned by her mother. She has been in therapy for the past two years.

Alan: Not currently. A suicide risk assessment was completed during the previous school year. At that time, Alan stated that he was depressed and thought about wanting to die or be killed. He reports that he no longer has those thoughts.

Question 5

Is the aggressive ideation focused on a specific, ongoing target?
Is there ongoing consideration of or focus on a particular person, group, or student body? If the situation lacks an ongoing target, it might be a situation of reactive aggression, in which the individual involved perceives himself or herself to be under immediate threat, is in an escalated emotional state, and uses threats as a means of self-protection or in defense of interests and wants. The situation also might be one of simple bravado or intimidation.

Daniel: No. Daniel's threat and aggressive behavior were focused on Will during a fight; however, it was determined that he does not have continuing focus or ideation on harming Will. The fight was an acute situation resulting from an argument.

Will: Yes. Will has held a grudge against Daniel since the sixth grade and considers Daniel someone who not only humiliates him on a regular basis and has stolen the one girlfriend Will thinks he will ever have but that Daniel's friends are also part of the motive and the vendetta. Both Daniel and his friends are specific and ongoing targets.

Alison: Yes. Al has communicated the intention to kill four students (Matt, John, Blake, and Maria) because of her perception of their ongoing bullying and harassment. She expresses intense anger and disgust with these students and their treatment of her.

Sam: No. Sam does focus his aggression on classroom and group home staff members, specifically on women between the ages of 25 and 40; however, he does not appear to be targeting anyone specifically. His behavior appears quite spontaneous and impulsive. The team attempts to identify the triggers that would cause him to focus on women in that particular age range.

Eric: Yes. Eric has clearly stated that he intends to cut or stab Kevin, Michael, Darren, and Jeff. Additionally, Eric says he will attack anyone else who tries to harm him or someone he cares about. He has also harmed Susan, his girlfriend, in a possible attempt to intimidate her. It is unclear at this point whether she is an ongoing target.

Maya: No. There is no indication that Maya has any specific or ongoing targets of aggression.

Alan: Yes. Alan stated that his targets are jocks and the student body. However, there is no indication that these are ongoing targets related to specific motives. He made the statement, but no other information supports that these are ongoing targets. His grandmother, on the other hand, does appear to be a source of ongoing anger and resentment, combined with longstanding violent ideation toward her.

Question 6

Are there indications of a choice and/or the availability of weapons?

If weapons are being considered but not immediately available within the home, are they available through relatives, friends, or other means? Note your level of confidence in the source of your information. Be sure to ask both the student and parents/guardians directly about weapons availability and document their responses.

Daniel: No. Daniel's parents report that they do not have any firearms in the home, and Daniel confirms this. The rifle that his father had was taken to Daniel's uncle's home. Daniel's parents did this because Daniel was very impulsive when he was in middle school, and they wanted to eliminate any possibility of danger. Daniel and his parents appear open and upfront about this information, so the team is confident in this information.

Will: Yes. Will's father reports that a .38 handgun was stolen, and Will admitted to having it in his possession. It was subsequently removed from his home during the law enforcement investigation, so Will no longer has access. Dale reported that Will has brought an unloaded firearm to school and was carrying it in the neighborhood. Will also would neither confirm nor deny that he had the weapon at school. Will has made a note to his friend Dale that he has everything he needs to seek revenge. He has done research on school shootings and written a short story involving the use of a rifle to seek revenge.

Alison: Yes. Al has access to a firearm and ammunition in her home and has practiced retrieving them from her parents' hiding spot. Her parents initially denied they had a gun but have since admitted they have a gun and have since given it to law enforcement to hold. Al has been clear that her plan involves shooting her targets. At this point, Al has weapons choice, but the weapon is not available to her. The team is confident in this information.

Sam: Yes. Supervisors in Sam's group home and within his classroom make every attempt to safeguard his environment. He does not have access to any traditional weapons. However, Sam is quite adept at finding weapons of opportunity, such as pencils, scissors, or heavy objects. Without a weapon, he will likely continue his aggressive behavior with his hands, attempting to strangle or beat others. Because of this, safety planning is critical.

Eric: Yes. Eric is in possession of a large lock-blade knife. In addition, Eric's mother stated that she would like to see him get a gun when he's old enough. Both Eric and his mother confirm this information.

Maya: Yes. Maya has a knife and sword collection, which her father is aware of and supervises. The collection is part of her gaming, and there is no indication that she intends to use these weapons to harm others.

Alan: No. In his communication, Alan has only discussed making bombs and using guns. He said that his father has a gun in his home but that it is secured in a safe, which was confirmed by his father. Alan and his father also go target shooting, but Alan does not have access to the firearm outside of that supervised activity. There are no firearms in his mother's home. The team is confident that his parents are being honest with this information. The team discussed firearm security with Alan's parents, and his father agreed to remove the firearm from his home and to discontinue target shooting with Alan.

Question 7

Are there indications of a focused or unusual interest in acts of violence, previous school or community attacks or attackers, weaponry, law enforcement or military paraphernalia or appearance, or antisocial characters, notorious criminals, murderers, or gangs (historical or fictional)? Are there indications of violent revenge fantasies or a desire to be an agent or martyr of a particular cause or belief system?

What might be inappropriate to some people still might be within the normal range, given the individual's age, developmental level, or cultural background. This question is similar to question No. 3. It examines whether interest is a curiosity or a fascination or whether interest is an admiration for antisocial characters as role models and examples of how to justify violence for solving problems.

Daniel: No. There are no instances reported of Daniel's admiring an antisocial or violent character. In fact, Daniel has quite positive relationships with his music teacher, math teacher, and scout leader, indicating his admiration for them as adults and leaders.

Will: Yes. Will has described an attack and has written a short story fantasizing about revenge. He has made references to his admiration for terrorists and mass shooters who have solved their problems by eliminating their adversaries and the popular, beautiful people on the planet through violent action. He also has written journal entries noting his admiration for vigilantes and other antisocial characters, both fictional and historical. Will has also researched Columbine and other school shootings on the internet.

Alison: Yes. In addition to specific references to her plans for a violent attack as revenge, Al's writings indicate that she sees herself as a martyr who will kill other students so they cannot harm others.

Sam: No. There is no indication that Sam identifies with other people who have acted out antisocially or violently. His behavior appears quite impulsive and is not rooted in an identification or a fixation with violent behavior or violent people.

Eric: Yes, to a degree. Eric identifies with special forces, but only as far as their hand-to-hand combat techniques. He is fixated on vigilantism and has rehearsed violent revenge fantasies.

Maya: No. Maya is immersed in fantasy play, but there are no indications of immersion in violence. Her role models are teachers, her father, and other prosocial adults.

Alan: Yes. Alan has a fascination with zombie apocalypse themes, violent video games, and books with violent themes. Alan states that he plays violent video games and watches zombie apocalypse videos because he wants to desensitize himself to death and enjoys the feeling of a fight-or-flight response. He also pursues violently themed literature.

Question 8

Are there indications of a motive that would justify the act of severely injuring another person?

If the focus is on a specific target or targets (see question No. 5), then there is very likely a motive. Motives tend to revolve around a person's need to establish or reestablish control. Motives might include revenge for humiliation or lost love, payback for a perceived injustice, revenge for bullying, a desire to kill, infamy, and the desire to establish power. If the situation is absent a motive, then it might be a situation that revolves around reactive aggression or the affectation of rage. Reactive aggressive talk often has triggers that agitate the situation rapidly.

Such triggers are usually not motives but should still be identified in order to avoid or eliminate them in the future. This question pairs with No. 5. If there is a focus on a specific target or targets, then there is very likely a motive.

Daniel: No. There is no evidence of any kind of thinking or ideation regarding targeted aggression. Additionally, an interview with Daniel suggested that he had remorse and was apologetic about the fight. Daniel also stated that he holds no grudges against Will and in fact thinks Will is a nice person.

Will: Yes. Will told a friend that Daniel stole his girlfriend and that Daniel and his friends have humiliated him over time. He has held a grudge against Daniel since the sixth grade. He has identified his motive, an ongoing grievance, in his handwritten journals and in his computer journal. He has made veiled references not only to his parents but also through his short story illustrating a vigilante attack by one character, Walter, against another character, David, for David's ongoing treachery and ruthless behavior.

Alison: Yes. Al's motive to harm her targets include grievances over bullying and harassment. Al has fixated on several situations in which she believes she was humiliated by her targets and was not supported by others involved.

Sam: No. While Sam's behavior is extremely aggressive, it is impulsive, with no indication of ongoing motive. Triggers and agitators of aggression will be addressed in the second portion of the Level 1 protocol.

Eric: Yes. Eric has had an ongoing grievance with his targets for the past three years. The grievance is the result of ongoing bullying and humiliation. Eric desperately wants to regain control and stand up for himself.

Maya: No. There is no indication of a motive for harming others.

Alan: Yes. There seems to be little grievance against peers at school, or any other indication of motive. However, Alan has ongoing resentment toward his grandmother for his perception of her emotional abuse of him. His ideation regarding harming her appears rooted in this motive.

Question 9

Are there indications of hopeless, overwhelming, stressful, or desperate situations (real or perceived)?

As students lose hope of resolving stressful or overwhelming situations through acceptable social or coping skills, they are more likely to engage in desperate solutions and last-ditch efforts to take control. Stressors might include humiliation, family conflict, mental illness, social distress, disciplinary actions, academic failure, law enforcement contact, bullying, etc. It is important to note that the point of this question is to examine the perception of the person or party with whom you are concerned, not necessarily what has been observed by others (e.g., staff members, parents, other students, or the community).

Daniel: No. Daniel reported that he was mostly happy and enjoyed school. His parents and his teachers confirmed that he seems to be a person with an optimistic attitude and a light heart. While Daniel has minor stressors, there have been no communications or indications that he is depressed or hopeless or that he feels overwhelmed.

Will: Yes. Will's father has been concerned for at least two years about Will's increasing withdrawal and depression. Will has a history of suicidal ideation, is disconnected from school and marginalized by peers, and is considering desperate solutions to his feelings of not belonging or being humiliated. Will refuses to meet with the counselor, and he is disconnected from all of the adults in his life. He has only one friend, who is a superficial relationship at best.

Alison: Yes. Al's communications suggest that she is experiencing intense stress and hopelessness. She reports feeling that she has gone crazy and needs mental health support. Al's stressors include difficult social relationships at school, bullying and harassment, pressure from her parents, and lack of hope for the future.

Sam: No. There is no indication that Sam is particularly hopeless or overwhelmed. When he is triggered, he does appear to be desperate; however, these situations are acute stressors and do not appear to create ongoing stress.

Eric: Yes. Historically, Eric is a victim of considerable abuse and trauma. He has withdrawn socially and academically. The humiliation and injury he has experienced from bullying, harassment, and abuse by multiple people in his life appear to be creating hypervigilance and the justification of violence as a solution. Furthermore, he does not see any alternatives to his problem with the boys at school.

Maya: No. Though Maya has experienced significant stressors historically, she is currently described as positive, with a strong group of friends. Maya has been in therapy for the past two years and is doing very well in school and at home.

Alan: Yes. Alan's mother reported that he's more stressed than usual regarding school, specifically his music activities. The team has some concerns about Alan's mental health, though his issues have not been documented diagnostically. The most significant stressor appears to be Alan's relationship with his grandmother and his perception that he cannot cope with contact with her.

Question 10

Are there indications of a capacity or ability to plan and carry out an act of targeted violence?

Based on the cognitive or adaptive capacity of the person or party of concern, what is the likelihood of a successfully organized and executed planned attack? If someone is making exaggerated or complex threats but is unable to organize and execute them because of supervision or a lack of cognitive ability or overall functioning, then feasibility drops.

Daniel: No. Daniel, as a human being, of course has the capacity to carry out a targeted violent attack if he intended to. However, there are no indications that he has an ongoing intention to hurt Will. He appears to have resolved the conflict and moved on and has no access to weapons.

Will: No. Though Will had access to a firearm and was conducting research to assist in executing the plan, the firearm has been removed from his possession and he is currently lodged in juvenile detention. Therefore, he currently has no ability to carry out an attack. However, the team is concerned that, without significant supervision, he might again access a weapon after his release from detention.

Alison: Yes. Though the firearm has been removed from her home, Al has made specific and detailed plans, and her parents have not been forthcoming about access to any other weapons.

Sam: No. Sam is very well supervised in his group home and within his classroom setting. Though Sam will weaponize any kind of material or object and use it aggressively toward another person in a reactive manner, his capacity and ability to plan and carry out a targeted attack are limited.

Eric: Yes. Eric has the capacity to act out his plan, as he has a weapon and has been practicing using it. He has stated that if his weapon is removed, he will find another.

Maya: No. Maya has no plan to act out aggressively.

Alan: No. While Alan has researched methods of a targeted attack, he does not currently have access to the weapons or materials needed, nor is it clear that he intends to follow through with this kind of attack.

Question 11

Are values, beliefs, or ideas socially maladjusted (e.g., aggression is seen as an acceptable and justifiable method of problem solving)?

Socially maladjusted thinking can lead to justification and motive for violent behavior. The thinking process will indicate thoughtful consideration that follows a process of reason and justification that is antisocial and intended to cause significant harm.

Unless it is accompanied by attack-related behavior (see question No. 3), communication or behavior that is a feature of a disability is less concerning than communication or behavior that is a feature of socially maladjusted thinking.

Daniel: No. Daniel's ideas and beliefs appear prosocial. He is positive about school, has strong relationships, and is trying to become a better problem solver and a less aggressive student.

Will: Yes. Journal entries, conversations, veiled comments, and information leakage suggest that Will has decided that violence is a reasonably acceptable method of solving his problems. This appears to be a desperate move to seek revenge on those who have humiliated him and whom he sees as contributors to his grievance and pain.

Alison: Yes. Al's communications indicate that she believes her planned attack will be reasonable revenge for the things the targets have done to her. She sees herself as a martyr who will avenge this situation, not just for her benefit but for the benefit of others as well.

Sam: No. Sam's disability involves considerable limits to his cognitive and adaptive functioning. Sam does not appear to be socially maladjusted or have values and beliefs that are antisocial. His communication is limited, and his thinking is often focused on the present moment. When or after Sam acts aggressively, he does not try to justify the act or even discuss it.

Eric: Yes. Eric claims to be fully justified in using violence as a solution. Eric's mother supports and even encourages his vigilante thinking as well as his justification to use violence as a solution.

Maya: No. Maya is a kind and friendly student who made a mistake in taking her new knives to school to show her fellow game players. She is remorseful and regrets her mistake but notes that she just couldn't resist showing them because the knives are so "cool."

Alan: No. While Alan has shared some atypical thoughts around the need for desensitization, he is generally a kind and caring person who engages in prosocial thinking.

Through a review of the first eleven questions of the Level 1 protocol, you can see how these questions assist the behavioral threat assessment team in consolidating the information that has been gathered, identifying risk factors, identifying protective factors, and beginning to lead the team to potential intervention strategies.

TEST YOURSELF

1. When a team is examining the context and situation of potential targeted violence, one important question to ask is:
    a. Does the person fit the profile of someone who would act out violently?

b. Does the person need a Snickers bar?
   c. Are there behavioral and circumstantial indications that a person poses a threat?
   d. Does the person have a mental health disorder that would cause violent behavior?
2. Reactive aggression is:
   a. Premeditated and impulsive.
   b. Highly emotional and predatory.
   c. Impulsive and affective.
3. Research strongly indicates that:
   a. Targeted violence attack-related behaviors move along a continuum from idea to plan to action.
   b. Evaluating mental illness plays a valuable role in determining violence potential.
   c. Targeted violence often results in an individual's just "snapping."
4. An example of a cultural script that exemplifies solving problems and getting even through violence is:
   a. The Columbine effect.
   b. *War and Peace* by Leo Tolstoy.
   c. The lyrics to "Poker Face" by Lady Gaga.
5. Two examples of warning signs that escalate the risk of targeted violence are:
   a. Preoccupation or fixation with a person or cause related to acts of targeted violence, previous school or community attacks, violent revenge, and/or violent extremist opinions.
   b. Talking politics with family during the holidays.
   c. Mental illness.
   d. Identification with school/mass shooters, antisocial characters and/or notorious violent criminals, and aggressive martyrdom.
6. The goal of the Level 1 protocol is to identify concerns, risk factors, and a lack of protective factors so you can:
   a. Refer the student to an outside professional who can help.
   b. Investigate the student's home life to determine whether the parents are at fault.
   c. Convince the student of concern that things aren't as bad as they seem.
   d. Address them with support, intervention, and prevention measures that decrease the escalating problem and deter the student from a trajectory toward violence.
7. When a team is examining youth aggression on a continuum of severity and frequency, it is important to:

a. Treat all types of aggression the same, with zero tolerance and harsh consequences.
b. Identify the "type" of student who would act out aggressively.
c. Understand the difference between low and moderate aggression, and extreme or violent aggression.

Answers: 1-c; 2-c; 3-a; 4-a; 5-a,d; 6-d; 7-c

Chapter 10

Question 12 as It Applies to the Seven Student Case Studies

After completing questions 1–11 in the Level 1 protocol, question 12, outlined below, determines the next course of action. This multipart question allows you to determine whether to continue with further questions or move directly to step 4 (chapter 13) and generate interventions.

Specifically, question 12 helps threat assessment teams differentiate between reactive and targeted aggression, determine the severity of the aggression (whether it is potentially violent or not), identify bravado and bullying, and dismiss benign language and rumors. This question also prompts teams to consider the potential impact of bias.

This chapter will present question 12, which contains four subquestions, noted as A–D. Then, as examples of collaborative discussion within the Level 1 teams, the chapter will present the answers for each of the seven case studies. Answers to the two subquestions regarding potential bias (both contained in A) will be discussed in chapter 12, Collaborative Decision Making.

QUESTION 12

Stop and review questions 1–11 and your responses to them. Highlight and identify responses where unintentional bias might have affected the response. Consider the following as you summarize the previous eleven questions:

   A. *Were any responses based on stereotypes or assumptions rather than on actual observation and factual information regarding behavior? Are there concerning behaviors that could be appropriate within the student's culture?* (In chapter 12, these two questions will be addressed in relation to each case study.)

B. *Do the responses identify actions, communications, and/or behaviors that suggest a motive focused on a specific target with an indication of planning or preparation, and the ability to carry out a targeted attack? If yes, proceed to question 13 (chapter 11).*
C. *Do the responses indicate either of the following: Aggressive talk or behavior that is highly emotional, is unplanned, and is a reaction to a perceived insult, affront, or threat, or a means of defending personal interest or self? Aggressive behavior and/or aggressive talk that is used to intimidate, bully, manipulate, or impress others? If yes to either question, the threat is likely reactive or affective. If the potential outcome of the aggression is serious or lethal injury, proceed with the assessment by moving on to question 13 (chapter 11). If the potential outcome of the aggression is minor to moderate injury, you may stop the assessment at this point and move on to prevention and intervention planning (chapter 13; step 4 in the Level 1 protocol), using the answers from questions 1–11 to identify situations, settings, and triggers that increase the likelihood of the behavior, and then develop strategies that will decrease that behavior.*
D. *If answers to the above items are no, the situation does not pose a threat. You may stop the assessment at this point and move on to prevention and intervention planning (chapter 13; step 4 in the Level 1 protocol), noting the absence of the threat under School Options: Other and continue to monitor the situation for behavior, ideas, or circumstances that might indicate the presence of risk.*

DANIEL

The team considers the presence of targeted aggression and concludes that there is no evidence of ongoing target, motive, or attack-related behavior in Daniel's original threat to shoot Will with his dad's shotgun (B). So, the answer to this question is no.

The question further asks whether the responses indicate aggressive talk or behavior that is highly emotional, unplanned, or in reaction to a perceived insult, affront, or threat, or a means of defending personal interest in this situation (C). Given that Daniel's threat occurred in the midst of a fight that he was losing, and appeared to be an expressive, emotional attempt to get Will to retreat, it appears to be a reactive gesture. Daniel confirmed this in his interview. Therefore, the answer to this question is yes.

Subquestion C further queries whether the aggressive behavior or aggressive talk is used to intimidate, bully, manipulate, or impress others. In this case, the answer is no. Daniel was behaving reactively and highly emotionally. He was not bullying or otherwise attempting to manipulate Will.

The final portion of subquestion C concerns the potential for serious injury. Because Daniel was identified as making a violent threat, but his behavior did not match the threat (the likely outcome of the fight would be moderate injury), the situation is identified as reactively aggressive with no indication of the potential for serious or lethal injury. Therefore, the team does not have to complete questions 13 through 20 and moves on to begin the intervention plan (chapter 13; step 4 in the Level 1 protocol).

WILL

Will does display several attack-related behaviors, including planning, rehearsal, target and location research, strongly determined motive, interest in vigilante justice, ongoing grievances, and weapons acquisition. In addition, he does appear to be out of options and sees very few solutions to his problems. So the answer to B is yes, which means the team proceeds with the assessment by moving on to question 13.

ALISON

Alison has identified four targets, has longstanding motive, and is displaying indications of attack-related behaviors, including planning, rehearsal, and acquisition of a weapon. She appears hopeless and out of options and has the ability to act out in a targeted, aggressive manner. The answer to subquestion B is yes, so the team proceeds with the assessment at question 13.

SAM

Then team considers subquestion B and determines that Sam does not have pre-identified targets, does not show evidence of motive for a targeted attack, and is not engaging in attack-related behaviors. Thus, the answer is no. Moving on to C, the team determines that Sam's behavior is highly emotional, unplanned, and in reaction to an immediate situation but is not an attempt to bully or manipulate. Furthermore, Sam's behavior does have the potential for serious or lethal injury, so the answer to the final portion of subquestion C is yes, and the team will proceed to question 13 (chapter 11).

ERIC

The team determines that Eric's situation indicates the potential for targeted aggression, because there are targets identified, strong evidence of motive, and signs of his engagement in attack-related behaviors, including planning, rehearsal, and the acquisition of a weapon. Eric's plan and his acceptance of the consequences are clear. Therefore, the answer to B is yes and the team moves on to question 13 (chapter 11).

MAYA

Answers to questions 1–11 indicate that Maya is not engaging in targeted aggression, so the answer to subquestion B is no. In addition, the team determines that she is not engaging in unplanned, highly emotional behavior, or behavior intended to bully or impress others, since she has made no communications or other indications that she intends to harm anyone. She simply brought knives to school as part of her gaming with her friends.

Therefore, the answers to B and C are no and the team determines that the situation does not pose a threat (subquestion D) and moves on to the intervention plan (chapter 13; step 4 in the Level 1 protocol) to determine whether she needs support as a result of the situation or whether restorative practices are needed as a result of the disruption caused in the school.

ALAN

The team considers the first subquestion and determines that while Alan does not appear to have ongoing targets at school, his grandmother does appear to be a potential target. Additionally, he has an established motive for acting out violently toward his grandmother. While the team is unclear about the actual presence or significance of the attack-related behavior that Alan highlighted in his social media posts, it is concerned about Alan's immersion in themes of violence and his intense anger toward his grandmother. Therefore, the team determines that the potential for targeted aggression is indicated (subquestion B) and moves on to question 13 (chapter 11).

The cases above are very different and highlight how this process addresses each situation as unique. One situation that can occur is bullying (not addressed within this book's case studies). Bullies tend to target vulnerable and easily intimidated peers and, as a result, often use extreme language and threats to inflate their status and cause fear.

Often these situations contain direct threats ranging from potentially moderately aggressive outcomes ("I'm going to beat you up if I see you after school") to potentially severe outcomes ("I'm going to kill you if I see you after school"). However, the language is almost always a feature of bravado and affectation, and the situations lack attack-related behavior. Bullies might injure others, but the intent is usually not to cause severe physical harm.

While bullying is problematic and causes considerable stress and fear with victims, it is addressed under subquestion C: "aggressive behavior and/or aggressive talk that is used to intimidate, bully, manipulate, or impress others." If the potential outcome of the aggression is serious or lethal injury, proceed with the assessment by moving on to question 13 (chapter 11).

If the potential outcome of the aggression is minor to moderate injury, you may stop the assessment at this point and move on to prevention and intervention planning (chapter 13; step 4 in the Level 1 protocol), using the answers from questions 1–11 to identify situations, settings, and triggers that increase the likelihood of the behavior, and then develop strategies that will decrease that behavior.

Situations involving bullying often necessitate a management plan to address the potential physical and psychological safety needs related to the behavior, which includes providing needed support to victims.

Chapter 11

Questions 13–20 as They Apply to Four of the Student Case Studies

After completing question 12 of the Level 1 protocol, for situations determined to include targeted aggression or reactive/affective aggression that might cause serious or lethal injury, the teams continue their Level 1 assessment by answering questions 13–20.

While questions 1–11, from chapter 9, assess the most critical situational factors related to targeted aggression, the intention of questions 13–20 is to form a more complete assessment of situations that have the potential for serious harm. This chapter will review questions 13–20, then answer each question regarding the five student situations that include this portion of the assessment. Both Daniel's and Maya's cases have moved on to step 4 in the Level 1 protocol (chapter 13).

SITE-BASED LEVEL 1 QUESTIONS 13–20

Question 13

Are caregivers, peers, and/or campus staff members concerned about the student's potential for acting out aggressively?

Concerns might range from an odd discomfort to a complete list of reasons that caution should be taken. If violence is being considered or planned, it is difficult to hide the indicators. In fact, sometimes little care is actually taken to hide intentions and while there might be little to no documentation of past behavioral issues, there might be several people who have been or are currently concerned.

Will: Yes. Multiple people have had considerable concern about Will. His school counselor and several teachers are concerned about his withdrawal from school. His relationship with his parents is very distressed. In fact, his parents have asked the police to take him because they don't believe they can handle his depression and rage. Additionally, his only, but superficial, friend, Dale, expressed concerns that he was not only worried about Will's aggression toward Daniel but that he might even become a target himself.

Alison: Yes. Prior to this assessment, school staff members were concerned about Al's attitude, but now that they have seen her recent communication, they are highly concerned about the potential for extreme aggression. Al's girlfriend is also concerned about her escalating anger toward and resentment of the four targeted students, so much so that she showed Al's note to school staff members. The perspective of Al's parents is unclear, as they appear to be deliberately withholding information.

Sam: Yes. As the team discussed this, it was clear that any teacher or staff member who has worked with Sam is very concerned about his potential for acting out aggressively because of the multiple instances of injury that have occurred. Sam's parents and group home staff are also concerned about the aggression he displays in the home setting.

Eric: Yes. Eric's school counselor, teachers, and girlfriend are all concerned about him. His mother is concerned about his past depression and dysfunction but is proud of his assertive move to become a man through violent solutions.

Alan: Yes, somewhat. School staff members are concerned about the incident last year that showed that Alan can be aggressive in a school setting; however, school staffers have not had concerns this year. Neither parent has been particularly concerned about Alan's behavior, though his mother has some reservations about his relationship with his grandmother. The team determined that prior to this incident others would have described Alan as doing well.

Question 14

Are there trusting and successful relationships with one or more responsible adults, either on campus or within the community?

The greater and healthier the connection with teachers, coaches, parents, administrators, church leaders, etc., then the less chance there is of a student's wanting to disappoint or hurt them and the greater opportunity there is for fostering positive values, community connections, and prosocial choices. If a student (or group of students) lacks connection to prosocial adults and is also marginalized within the student population, then intervention and connection are strongly indicated.

Will: No. Will has no relationships or connections with adults in the school or the community, and his relationship with his parents is very distressed. Will is disconnected. He has very little, if any, interest in the institution of education or care or regard for the adult staff members who work in the school.

Alison: Yes. Al has identified both her adult sister and her mother's friend Teressa as adults whom she can trust and confide in. She has few positive adult connections at school but has some relationship with her school counselor that could be strengthened.

Sam: Yes. Sam's most successful connections are with male or female staff members over the age of 40 or 45. While these relationships are fairly superficial, Sam is responsive to staff members who fit that description and is able to discuss his day and stressful events in a constructive manner.

Eric: No. Eric is completely marginalized and has no connections with school staff members or other prosocial adults.

Alan: Yes. Alan gets along well with his teachers, and he identified the ones he likes. Many teachers enjoy his participation in class, although some are concerned about his stress level and the pressure he places on himself regarding his musical endeavors. He also has a particularly positive and trusting relationship with his father, who appears prosocial and supportive.

Question 15

What circumstances, events, or triggers increase or agitate the likelihood of a violent or aggressive attack?

What information or developments might increase the concern for acted-out aggression? Which situations agitate or trigger aggressive thinking, threats, and behavior? Is there an indication that the student or students of concern are awaiting an event or action before making their final decision regarding violent behavior?

> Will: Humiliation, teasing, and rejection are significant triggers for Will. He appears to have decided that he is not going to stand for his status in school any longer. It might be prudent to consider the next situation, fight, or rejection as an acute trigger that could cause Will to act out, if he is not already preparing to do so at this point.

> Alison: Al has stated that she will put her plan for violence into motion if she can't contact her two supports (her sister and Teressa) and if one of the targeted students insults her or "pulls a smart comment." Al appears to misperceive social situations, so what appears insulting to her might not be noticed or identified as concerning by others. Any contact with or perceived rejection by these students is a likely trigger.

> Sam: When the team examined the circumstances and a previously completed functional behavioral assessment, it became clear that Sam was easily agitated by any kind of excessive noise, especially if he was in the vicinity of someone who appeared to be female and between the ages of about 25 and 40.

> Eric: Eric is very clear that triggers include any bullying or humiliation. His circumstances also suggest that failure, abuse, and rejection are potential triggers or accelerators as well.

> Alan: The one identifiable trigger is any contact with his grandmother.

Question 16

What circumstances, events, or inhibitors <u>decrease</u> the likelihood of a violent or aggressive attack?

What information or developments might decrease the concern for acted-out aggression? Identify all positive influences (e.g., activities, events, interests, relationships, goals, organization memberships, etc.) that promote responsible and accountable prosocial behavior. A situation that lacks inhibitors poses a greater risk, since a student has less to lose by acting out and little motivation toward healthy solutions.

Will: The team is unable to determine any inhibitors or protective factors that are present in Will's life at this point. Will's father did recall that when Will was in the seventh grade, he learned to play the guitar and very much enjoyed it. Will had a music teacher when he was a freshman who noted on a teacher survey that Will had come into high school happy to be a musician. However, by his sophomore year, he seemed to have lost interest in playing the guitar and became quite unresponsive when asked to join the school band.

Additionally, when Will was in elementary school, he loved to make art and his academic record is full of notations of his creativity. Though these are not current inhibitors, they are potential options for building positive experiences in the future.

Alison: Al's relationships with her sister, mother's friend, and girlfriend are inhibitors, as they are all very important to her and seen as trusted confidants. In addition, Al is a gifted student who can identify goals that include moving to New York, going to college, and living on her own. Allowing no contact with the targeted students will likely reduce the concern for aggression.

Sam: The team examined the circumstances and a previously completed functional behavioral assessment and determined that inhibitors and protective factors included Sam's being in a calm and quiet environment, interacting with older school and group home staffers, and interacting with staff members who used a parallel interactive process that was not directly engaging.

Eric: The team was not able to identify current inhibitors or protective factors for Eric. Developments that would decrease the concerns for violence include an end to the bullying and connection with a positive, prosocial role model. The team also hopes that the students identified as bullies will apologize to Eric, as this could be a strong inhibitor.

Alan: Alan has multiple inhibitors. He is involved in band and choir, has a group of prosocial friends at school, is involved in a church youth group, respects his teachers and their opinions, and has a strong relationship with his father.

Question 17

Are there indications that the peer group reinforces delinquent thinking?

106   Chapter 11

Are there peer relationships, marginalized peer-group status, and/or peer-accepted delinquent thinking to support the use of violence as a solution? Risk increases if a situation lacks positive social connection, accountability, and inhibitors and is filled with antisocial thinking about entitlement, revenge, and the use of violence as an acceptable means of solving problems.

Will: No. Will is quite disconnected from his peers, and his only relationship, which is superficial, is with Dale. The team does not believe that Dale was reinforcing of Will's ideas of revenge. In fact, Dale denied being a part of any of the thinking and even insisted that he was not really Will's friend.

Alison: No. Al's only friend is her girlfriend, who does not appear to be supportive of Al's plans for violence and is concerned about her. She initially resisted giving the school information about Al but then cooperated and provided information about her concerns.

Sam: No. Sam is not socially connected to other students and does not have a peer group or a friend whom he relates well to. Sam's relationships are mostly with adults.

Eric: Yes. Eric's peer group is actually his mother. She is more of a friend than a parent, and she supports extreme aggression as a problem-solving strategy.

Alan: Yes. The group message string on social media that he was part of was engaging in negative, offensive, and provocative talk. There were other students referenced who have expressed negative or violent thinking. It does not appear that Alan spends time in person with these students, but his communication with them on social media could increase his consideration of aggressive solutions.

Question 18

Is there a history of behavioral, drug or alcohol, or developmental issues?
Are there issues related to vulnerability and coping skills not necessarily directly related to targeted aggression? Risk increases considerably when coping strategies are limited.

Will: Some concern. Will's father noted that when Will was in the eighth and ninth grades, he was able to purchase alcohol on several occasions through an adult and was caught drinking in his room. Will's father said Will rarely leaves the house now and almost never socializes, and he does not suspect that Will is drinking or using drugs. While Will has not had significant behavior problems at school, he has a history of academic and social failure.

Alison: Yes. While there is no indication of drug and alcohol use, or developmental issues, Al has historically experienced significant challenges socially. Since elementary school, she has struggled with making friends and maintaining relationships and has a history of misinterpreting social cues.

Sam: Yes. Sam does have developmental issues and a disability related to both cognitive and adaptive delays.

Eric: Yes. Eric's academic functioning has been flat for the past two years. He is credit deficient and often truant from school. His coping skills have been mostly withdrawal and retreat, until this recent change in attitude and acceptance of aggression as a solution.

Alan: Some. Alan has had a few referrals for oppositional behavior; however, nothing that is beyond typical adolescent behavior. Alan was referred for a psychoeducational evaluation in elementary school over concerns that his ADHD diagnosis and characteristics of autism spectrum disorder were interfering with his educational progress. But his parents decided to decline the completion of the process, stating that his problems were the result of their divorce and that they were addressing the issues through private counseling.

Question 19

Are there issues that indicate a low reserve of coping strategies and a lack of emotional resiliency?

Will: Yes. Will has poor and lacking coping skills. He is clearly emotionally distressed and has very little resiliency in the face of any kind of teasing or humiliation. In fact, Will is an injustice collector who is focusing intensely on revenge for all of the harm and offensive behavior that he has experienced.

Alison: Yes. Al's communications suggest that she is highly distressed and overwhelmed and believes that violence might be one of the only solutions she has left. She has a history of difficulty coping with social stressors.

Sam: Yes. When discussing Sam, his disabilities, and the kinds of social issues that are interfering with his success, the team determined that he does lack coping strategies and emotional resiliency. Sam's cognitive and adaptive delays place his development several years behind his chronological age.

Eric: Yes. Eric witnessed considerable domestic abuse from his stepfather directed at his mother. He feels that he failed his mother and is determined to protect her, himself, and his girlfriend from now on, even if it means stabbing or killing someone. He is unable or unwilling to consider coping strategies that do not include aggression.

Alan: Yes. While Alan functions relatively well in school, he has little ability to cope with the relationship with his grandmother. He has attempted several coping strategies, but they have failed. His mother disclosed that he struggled with depression last year and was able to see a counselor. This seemed to help quite a bit. She is also concerned about his anxiety regarding his relationship with his grandmother and his musical ambition.

Question 20

Other Concerns:

The Level 1 protocol is not a fixed checklist and does not provide a quantifiable score or level of risk. It is intended as a set of pertinent questions that encourage discussion and examination of concerns. Are there other concerns not noted elsewhere in this survey? Examples might include sexual misconduct, fire play, animal abuse, exposure to domestic violence, criminal behavior, etc.

Will: The team suspects that Will might be experiencing depression. Although Will has not been diagnosed or treated, his withdrawal and deterioration in functioning are significant. The team noted that Will historically has been exposed to considerable teasing and humiliation by his peers. In addition, Will has a history of being concerned about his family's financial situation and his lack of nice clothing, as well as his inability to participate in activities because of the family's income instability.

Alison: The team believes that Al's romantic relationship with Alex is her first relationship with a female. Although Al seems to misperceive social interactions, there is potential that Al has experienced bullying or harassment related to her sexuality. The team notes that it will investigate this further. In addition, Al also seems to be experiencing signs of depression.

Sam: Prior to the group home placement, Sam had been exposed to domestic violence, criminal behavior in his home, and considerable neglect.

Eric: Eric and his mother are resistant to intervention at this point. They claim that they will be fine and believe that Eric will be exonerated on grounds of self-defense should he act out violently. Their thinking is skewed, but team members have not been able to convince them that Eric is in danger of arrest and detention.

Alan: Alan is a bit of a prankster and a joker (which can be disruptive to the class), but overall, he is a good student, respectful to adults, and does not engage in conflict with peers.

While questions 1–11 from chapter 9 assessed the most critical situational factors related to targeted aggression, this chapter has highlighted questions 13–20, allowing the threat assessment teams to form a more complete assessment of situations that have the potential for serious harm. The following chapters will complete the assessment through collaborative decision making (chapter 12) and reversing the pathway through building intervention plans that embrace connection, restorative practice, building protective factors, and keeping all students safe (chapter 13).

TEST YOURSELF

1. Triggers tend to be:
   a. Acute situations or events that quickly escalate a situation to potential aggression or violence.
   b. Small, curved, metal devices that activate a weapon.
   c. Events that cause teachers to take up smoking.
2. Inhibitors or protective factors are:
   a. Embarrassing situations that cause a student to be withdrawn and shy.

b. Surveillance systems, metal detectors, and junkyard dogs patrolling the school grounds.
   c. Circumstances, activities, relationships, and motivations that decrease the likelihood of a student's acting out.
3. Trusting and successful relationships with prosocial adults are important for two of the following reasons:
   a. Prosocial adults can help students consider positive choices.
   b. Adults can help them get into the right college.
   c. These adults can tell the students' parents when they do something wrong.
   d. Adults can assist in making healthy connections in the community.

Answers: 1-a; 2-c; 3-a

PART IV
Complete the Process

Chapter 12

Collaborative Decision Making

After completing the assessment questions, the team then engages in a collaborative discussion to articulate the members' concerns and take precautionary measures to protect against any imminent danger. The team also engages in a discussion regarding the potential for bias and cultural considerations that might affect the assessment.

This discussion assists the team in distilling its concerns to the most pressing ones and setting the stage for the development of a management plan. This chapter lists the discussion topics as stated in the Level 1 protocol, then briefly summarizes the discussions had by each threat assessment team, as well as the precautionary steps taken, regarding the seven case studies.

Instructions (from the Level 1 protocol, see the appendix and Questions for Team Discussion)

1. Were any responses to the Level 1 protocol questions based on stereotypes or assumptions rather than on actual observation and factual information regarding behavior? Are there concerning behaviors that could be appropriate within a student's culture?
2. Review all previous questions and highlight/identify responses that indicate concern.
3. Identify your impressions and sense of urgency.
4. Is the potential aggression likely to cause severe or lethal injury?
5. Do the responses identify threats (i.e., actions, specific circumstances, and/or communications) that are focused on a specific target (i.e., an individual or a group) for a specific reason or motive, and do any of the threats involve planning and preparation, with the student's capacity to carry out the event? If so, concern for targeted aggression is indicated and must be addressed immediately.
6. Is there any indication that an attack has been scheduled, or is there an identified date when an attack might happen?

7. Take immediate precautionary measures to protect potential victims and ensure supervision for the student or students of concern if:
   - Targeted aggression is indicated.
   - Potential victims are identified.
   - The potential outcome of the aggression might cause severe or lethal injury.

Precautionary measures might include but are not limited to:

- If there is any concern about imminent violence or if anyone is in immediate danger, call law enforcement (911).
- Contact district administration and safety/security services for consultation and support.
- Contact the student threat assessment team (STAT) for further assessment, consultation, and support.
- Notify the guardians of the potential target or targets of your concerns and the actions you are initiating. Document all communication using the Notification Log and Notification Letter (see the appendix). Outline and document a safety plan for the targeted student or students (see the appendix).
- Consider all options available to inhibit or decrease the chances of violence. Proceed to the intervention plan for a partial list of options that are available within the district. Options also might include restricting access to the target, targets, or campus; however, it is important to remember that removing any student or students who pose a threat does not necessarily decrease that threat if the students are not supervised when away from campus. Since the use of suspension or expulsion might actually increase risk, the resulting elevated risk should be factored into the assessment.

DANIEL

The team begins the discussion by considering the potential for bias or the impact of culture on Daniel's behavior. Team members know Daniel to be an impulsive, occasionally aggressive student, but they focused their responses on Daniel's behavior and communications during and after the fight, as well as the information they gathered from other sources.

Therefore, they base their responses on facts and behavior rather than on assumptions. Daniel is a bilingual Mexican-American student, and there is no indication that the threat he made is appropriate within his culture. In fact, his parents strongly disapproved of his behavior, and they support the school's process of assessment, prevention, and application of consequences.

The team determines that Daniel's communication was an impulsive threat made to end the fight and, therefore, was a situation of reactive aggression. Outside of the threat made during the fight, there is no evidence of other situational factors of concern for targeted aggression, and there is no need for precautionary measures. Since Daniel might engage in reactive aggression or fighting in the future, the team will move on to building an intervention plan (chapter 13; step 4 in the Level 1 protocol) and focus on strategies to assist Daniel in developing coping skills and alternatives to fighting.

WILL

The team discusses potential bias and determines that all of the information it considered was based on Will's observed behavior and communication. Team members also determine that Will's behavior and communication are objectively concerning and would not be appropriate within the context of any culture.

The potential for targeted aggression is identified, along with targets, as well as the presence of planning, research, preparation, rehearsal, perceived lack of alternatives, hopelessness, acquisition of a weapon, and the potential for lethal injury. Because of all of these factors, the situation is considered urgent and requires precautionary measures.

Will has been arrested and lodged in detention because of the gun theft and subsequent possession of the gun in school, so the team has some time to develop a plan; however, since he will likely be released to his parents' supervision, the team decides to work with the assigned juvenile services worker to quickly implement the plan, which will include notification of the school when Will is released.

Given the significant level of concern, the team works with the law enforcement officer to provide Daniel's parents and the students named as targets with the information necessary to clearly identify the danger, implement protective strategies, and schedule meetings with them to develop safety plans for their children (an example can be found through a link in the appendix).

Finally, the team knows that Will is likely to be expelled for bringing the gun to school and realizes that his distress might increase as a result. Including the juvenile services case worker, the music and art teachers (since he had previously been interested in those subjects), and Will's parents in the intervention (chapter 13; Level 1, step 4) will be key to building a plan that will support him at the alternative education school and in the community.

ALISON

The team considers whether bias was involved in the assessment, with particular attention to Al's sexual orientation. The team reviews its answers to the assessment questions and determines that the answers were based on facts regarding Al's communications and behavior. The team then considers the potential that Al has been bullied or harassed because of her sexuality.

Team members determine that the concern for targeted aggression is significant, regardless of the origin of the motive; however, they decide that they will investigate the bullying further to determine whether they need to take any additional steps with the targeted students or whether there are culturally responsive supports that could be provided to Al.

The team identifies significant concerns for targeted aggression, including the naming of targets, the potential for lethal injury, a well-thought-out plan, access to a weapon, severe stress and hopelessness, and a willingness to complete suicide as the final component of the plan. Though Al has been taken into custody and the weapon has been removed from her home, the situation is still in need of significant supports, since Al will be released to the custody of her parents, who have not been forthcoming with the team.

The team determines that it will notify district administration and the district threat assessment lead for additional support. It also works with law enforcement to notify the parents or guardians of the targeted students.

In this case, because of the clear risk, team members will provide potential victims' parents or guardians with the information necessary to support the safety of their children. They make a plan to meet with these parents individually to develop safety plans. The team will move forward with the intervention plan (chapter 13; step 4 in the Level 1 protocol) needed to maintain safety and support Al.

SAM

Sam is a student with multiple disabilities. Team members discuss whether their responses were due to any stereotypes or assumptions based on his identity or his disability and conclude that their responses were based only on observable acted-out behavior. His behavior is due to disability rather than cultural expectations. The team discusses the need to respond to Sam's behavior in an inclusive, supportive, and nonpunitive manner, with the support of his IEP team.

The team determines that Sam's behavior is a result of reactive aggression, not targeted, but has caused, and will likely continue to cause, serious injury.

Team members believe there is a potential for ongoing serious aggression but believe that immediate precautionary measures are not necessary. The team will move forward with the intervention plan (chapter 13; step 4 in the Level 1 protocol) and identify strategies to maintain safety in Sam's environments, reduce triggers for aggression, and provide any other needed intervention.

ERIC

The team considers whether any assumptions or stereotypes played into the assessment of Eric's situation. Members review their responses and agree that the assessment was based on factual information, including Eric's own responses, and his girlfriend's and mother's perspectives. They also consider whether Eric's behavior might be appropriate within his culture. Eric identifies as Asian-American.

The team, which includes an Asian-American instructional assistant, determines that while his behavior does not appear to be appropriate within his culture, it is supported by his mother. The team considers that Eric's mother might benefit from culturally responsive support and culturally relevant connections to support her own well-being and makes note to consider this in management planning.

The assessment questions indicate that there are concerns related to identified targets, strong motive, perceived lack of alternatives, willingness to accept the consequences of violence, acquisition of a weapon, and clearly stated planning and preparation. The team believes this to be an urgent situation that has the potential for serious or lethal injury, which Eric states could take place in the next two to three weeks.

Because of this, the team determines that it needs to contact the district administration and the district threat assessment lead for extra support. The team also decides to notify the parents or guardians of the targeted students and inform them of the danger.

In addition, Eric believes that no one can help him solve his problem of being bullied by the other students. The team concludes that it needs to find a way to stop the bullying and convince the students involved that they must take accountability for their actions. It will determine how to approach this when discussing the management plan.

MAYA

In assessing potential bias, the team discusses whether any members might have dismissed concerns for aggression because Maya is such a well-liked student. Members review their answers and determine that, while Maya is indeed likable, their answers were based on objective and factual information that was corroborated by multiple sources.

The team concludes that there is no concern for either targeted or reactive aggression, so it will move forward to determine whether the situation needs any intervention (chapter 13; step 4 in the Level 1 protocol).

ALAN

Alan identifies as a Hispanic student. The team discusses whether his cultural identity led to any stereotypes or assumptions during this assessment. The team believes its responses were based on observations and factual information gathered, but it does consider whether Alan's strained relationship with his grandmother has any cultural significance. One administrator on the team is also Hispanic and spoke of normal extended family relationships within Hispanic and Latino families, leading the team to determine that Alan's response to this relationship is not a typical feature of his culture.

The team discusses Alan's case and has identified its concerns. Members do not believe there is an ongoing target in the school or indications of motive and attack-related behavior related to the school setting. Furthermore, Alan has strong relationships and multiple inhibitors, and he generally appears to be doing well socially, academically, and behaviorally.

However, Alan's intense anger and previous consideration of harming his grandmother are very concerning, although the team did not identify any current attack-related behavior connected to her as a potential target. The team decides to contact the district threat assessment lead to clarify these concerns and determine a course of action through the intervention plan (chapter 13; step 4 in the Level 1 protocol).

Multidisciplinary behavioral threat assessment is a leading practice in violence prevention, in part because of the opportunity for assessment and decision making by a group of professionals with varied roles, information, and perspectives teaming with parents and guardians. Engaging in collaborative discussion displays the benefits of this approach, as all members have the opportunity to express their perspectives and no one individual bears the weight of the decisions being made.

This discussion guides teams toward developing the most effective management plan for the situations they have efficiently and thoroughly assessed.

TEST YOURSELF

1. Precautionary measures are needed in three of the following situations:
   a. Potential victims are identified.
   b. Threat is reactive.
   c. Targeted aggression is indicated.
   d. The potential outcome might include serious or lethal injury.
   e. Aggression is reactive and poses no risk of serious harm.
2. If targeted aggression is identified, precautionary measures might include:
   a. Notifying the parents or guardians of potential targets.
   b. Suspension of the students of concern in order to teach them a lesson.
   c. Notifying the media of the concern.
3. Collaborative team discussion should consist of all of the following except:
   a. Discussion of the potential for targeted aggression.
   b. Identification of potential bias and the impact of culture on behavior.
   c. Discussion regarding the potential for serious or lethal injury.
   d. Identification of mental health providers who can evaluate students who make threats.

Answers: 1-a,c,d; 2-a; 3-d

Chapter 13

Managing Cases with Prevention, Inclusion, and Connection

After a team engages in a thorough assessment of a situation and conducts a collaborative discussion about its conclusions, developing management strategies is the next and most important step. Determining the most appropriate management strategies—those that fit the situation and do not underreact or overreact to the situation—is the art of behavioral threat assessment and management.

A critical misstep that teams might make is completing a thorough assessment but then engaging in a lackluster approach to management, either creating a minimal plan or none at all and/or failing to follow up on student progress over time. Creating an appropriate plan and monitoring progress until all safety concerns have been resolved are critical for maintaining safety and supporting students.

This chapter will provide an overview of case management options and discuss the elements that drive a referral for a Level 2 assessment. Then, using the seven previously outlined case studies as examples, the chapter will provide a summary of the management plans created by threat assessment teams that used the intervention options listed in step 4 of the Level 1 protocol linked in the appendix. Schools or districts that are implementing the Level 1 process should review and edit that list to include additional options that are available in their communities.

While recalling the case studies reviewed in the previous chapters, refer to the options noted in the step 4 list and consider the following general management strategies as your guide:

- *Protect the potential target.* This should always be the priority. Consider your notification responsibilities and consider completing a Plan to Protect the Targeted Student (see the appendix). Strategies might include limiting contact between the student of concern and the target, providing

information to the targeted person on how to report concerns, providing connections to adults who can support the targeted person, safety planning, or involving a domestic violence or victim's advocate.
- *Increase accountability.* Consider using a restorative practice approach to creating an accountability plan for the student of concern, outlining behavioral expectations, identifying supports the student will receive, and informing the student of the consequences of problematic behavior. If a student is able to accept accountability and follow through with the management plan, the student also might accept the opportunity to implement restorative justice strategies, and your concern will likely decrease. If a student is not able to accept accountability and is unwilling to follow planning steps, your concern might increase.
- *Increase supervision.* Consider school, home, and community supervision needs. At school, needs can vary based on the type of setting (e.g., highly structured vs. less structured). Provide parents and guardians with recommendations on supervision at home and in the community. Consider engaging in scenario planning, in which your team brainstorms potentially concerning situations based upon known risk factors and plans accordingly. The question to ask is: Have you done everything you can do to keep everyone involved safe?
- *Limit all access to weapons.* Parents and guardians might need support in understanding how to secure or remove weapons from the home (the law enforcement member of your team is likely a great resource to advise and guide parents and guardians). When there are concerns about a student bringing a weapon to school, consider conducting intermittent checks of belongings completed by trusted staff members (intermittent checks of belongings tend to be most effective because they cannot be predicted). To show respect for the student, safety checks should be done in private, as a restorative justice intervention.
- *Monitor communications.* Consider methods of monitoring student communication, whether it is oral or written and whether it is expressed through social media or any other means. Provide information on red flags to those who can monitor communications and tell them how and when to report. Remember that peers are often aware of concerns about violence, so determine how best to monitor peer concerns.
- *Build relationships.* This is the most important intervention for all at-risk students. Find at least one prosocial adult working within the school who can meet with the student on a regular basis to develop a trusting relationship. Use natural connections whenever possible and consider the need for culturally relevant connections. This is an area where restorative justice can shine because the relationships will be focused not on the problematic behavior, discipline, or academic expectations

but rather on moving forward, building trust, and maintaining a healthy perspective.
- *Increase protective factors (inhibitors).* These will be unique to every situation. Potential inhibitors are structured activities, peer relationships, family support, clubs, activities, sports, music, art, and other creative endeavors or constructive interests. Other resources that might assist the student are peer support programs, therapeutic counseling, life skills classes, tutoring in specific academic subjects, or mental health care—all of which enhance social learning and emotional competency. Most of these programs and supports will be available within the school, but the team also might need to access community resources to assist with managing, monitoring, and building relationships.
- *Decrease agitators.* As with protective factors, these will be unique to each situation. Consider creative methods for reducing stressors and engineer the student's environment around known or suspected agitators. Often, the team will determine that the student is not currently at risk for engaging in violence but requires monitoring or is in need of guidance to cope with losses, develop resilience to overcome setbacks, or learn more appropriate strategies to manage emotions.
- *Remove or redirect the student's motive.* Every student's motive will be different, and motives can be redirected in a variety of ways. These strategies might include bullying prevention efforts or counseling for a student experiencing a personal setback. Address and solve root causes if those are determined.
- *Explore community resources.* Community support options are the strength of the Level 2 (community-based) team; however, Level 1 teams are likely to have knowledge of many community options as well. Options to consider include mental health treatment, wraparound support, involvement in a faith community, mentorship options, preventive services offered by juvenile justice agencies, music and theater programs, sports and clubs, LGBTQ advocacy groups, BIPOC support programs, domestic violence prevention support, etc.
- *Removal of student (last resort).* Sometimes management involves a student's suspension or expulsion from school. When this is necessary, teams and school administrators should consider how it might affect their ability to monitor the student. Removing a student from school does not eliminate the risk to the school community. Several school attacks have been carried out by students who had been removed from school or aged out of their former schools. A suspended or expelled student might become isolated from positive peer interactions or supportive adult relationships at school. Furthermore, as chapter 2 noted, expulsion often causes increased risk of incarceration and recidivism. Teams

should develop strategies to stay connected to the suspended or expelled student so they can respond appropriately if the student's situation is deteriorating or the behaviors of concern are escalating. If a student is removed from school, the team must do everything it can to build and maintain positive relationships.

Above all, management plans need to maintain safety but must respect the dignity of everyone involved. Any plan that introduces or increases shame or humiliation in a student's life is likely to increase both concern for potential aggression and an array of negative life outcomes.

The last decision that teams will make in the Level 1 process is a determination of whether to refer a situation for Level 2 (community) assessment. A case can be referred to the Level 2 team to gain further support, for additional investigation, and to pursue resources that will assist with prevention. The following are considerations for Level 2 referral:

- Your team has concerns regarding extreme aggression but is unable to confidently answer the questions from chapters 9–11 (from the Level 1 assessment protocol).
- Your team confidently answered the questions from chapters 9–11 (from the Level 1 assessment protocol) and has safety concerns regarding impulsive or reactive behavior that will likely result in serious or lethal injury to another.
- Your team has confidently answered the questions from chapters 9–11 (from the Level 1 assessment protocol) and has concerns regarding threats of targeted aggression that indicate motive, plan, preparation, scheduling, and/or other behavior that suggests the serious consideration of an act of targeted aggression.
- Your team has exhausted its building resources and would like to explore community support to assist with intervention, management, and supervision.
- A student has brought a gun to school, attempted to acquire a gun with intent to harm or intimidate others, or has been arrested for firearm-related offenses in the community.

THREAT MANAGEMENT PLANS FOR SEVEN CASE STUDIES

The following is a summary of the management plans developed for each of the seven student case studies presented in earlier chapters. Note that several of these cases were referred for Level 2 assessment; in those cases, the management plans developed were a synthesis of strategies recommended by both the Level 1 and Level 2 teams.

DANIEL

Daniel's situation was determined to be moderately aggressive, and his behavior was deemed to be a display of reactive aggression. Schools are fairly well set up to deal with aggressive, impulsive youths who sometimes fight, so the intervention strategies follow a fairly typical route. Daniel did make a threat of violence, so notification to Will's parents is required. In this situation, the school administrator provides basic information about the threat as part of her interview with the parents regarding Will's behavior. In addition, both a teacher and another student's parent heard Daniel's threat and were frightened, so the administrator contacts them both to tell them that the school has engaged the threat assessment system, which identifies risk factors for targeted aggression and has a plan in place to maintain safety.

The team decides to develop an accountability plan that requires Daniel to monitor his impulsive behavior, anger, and coping skills, and provides him with a route to a school counselor or a teacher mentor if he needs assistance with processing prosocial and nonaggressive ways of solving his problems. The team also refers Daniel to its multitiered systems of support (MTSS) team to assist him in his efforts to compensate for his ADHD diagnosis. The team considers recommending a referral for a Section 504 or special education evaluation.

Because Daniel made a concerning threat, the team decides to monitor his communications for ongoing concerns and for agitating experiences so they can be addressed when they occur. The school counselor will provide a weekly check-in with Daniel and work with him on developing prosocial options to his problems and to continue building a positive relationship with him.

One of the initial check-ins will include a discussion about how Daniel's threats were frightening to some of the people who witnessed the fight. The counselor will offer Daniel the opportunity to sit down with those affected so he can hear their concerns and apologize for the fear caused by his behavior.

The team agrees that Daniel's parents are doing an excellent job of supervising him and have accessed support through a private counselor. Considering Daniel's father's report that their cultural heritage is very important to the family, the team offers Daniel's parents the option of a referral to a counselor who shares their ethnicity. In fact, the school has a mental health partnership with a local agency that provides mental health support at the school, and the primary counselor is also Mexican-American. Daniel's father believes that this would be a very positive option for his son and states that he will contact the provider.

The school counselor will also check in with Daniel's parents on a regular basis to make sure that they are supported and to open communication between school and home regarding particular problems that Daniel might be experiencing that would increase his tendency to be impulsive and act out.

The team determines that a referral for Level 2 assessment is not necessary, as Daniel's behavior is reactive and not likely to result in serious injury. The team believes it can manage the situation using school resources.

Last, the team identifies a review date when the administrator can check in with teachers, parents, and others who are involved with Daniel to determine whether the supervision strategies and the intervention plan are working or need to be modified.

WILL

Because of the significant risk factors for targeted aggression and the potential for violence, the team decides to refer Will's case for a Level 2 assessment. The following is a discussion of strategies by both the Level 1 and Level 2 teams, Will's parents, the district threat assessment lead, a law enforcement officer, a public mental health specialist, and the assigned probation officer.

The team begins discussion of the management options by stressing that Will is brittle and sensitive, so they must honor his dignity through this process. They agree that this cannot be a punitive process. Although they are very concerned about the violence Will is considering and the possible criminal repercussions, they must foster as trusting a relationship as possible.

To begin, there are multiple targets identified and the team is concerned about the possibility of violence. Team members determine that the parents or guardians of those students will need to be notified and, because the situation is so concerning and the parents or guardians need the information to protect their children, they will need the details necessary to keep their children safe.

Given the sensitive nature of this situation, the team asks its law enforcement representative to assist with those contacts and talk to the parents about safety and protective strategies. Team members also decide that they will offer to meet with the parents or guardians individually to develop school-based safety plans. Since Will is likely to be expelled for possessing a firearm at school, he will not be in contact with Daniel or the other targeted students at school, but an additional plan will need to be made for limiting all contact in the community.

In addition, the team works with the district security department to provide extra support to the school during the assessment and immediate intervention stage of safety planning. Since the local shopping mall is also a potential target, the law enforcement officer works with mall security on monitoring any suspicious activity there.

Will is arrested and is suspended pending expulsion (for possessing a firearm at school), so the team discusses the need for supervision and an infusion of support throughout this process. Because of the potential expulsion, the administrator of the local alternative program is also in attendance at this meeting. The team discusses options for Will's placement in that program. The probation officer involved in this case also explains that school attendance will be a part of Will's conditional release, so organizing his immediate admission to the alternative program will be important.

The team discusses Will's emotional state and his depressed functioning at school and at home. As a result, the team recommends a referral to the MTSS to consider the need for a special education or Section 504 evaluation. The team recommends that school administrators monitor Will's communications (oral, written, and social media) and encourage his parents to do the same.

The team recommends a daily check of Will's belongings, when he is back in school, which will change to an intermittent schedule once he is settled in. For that role, the team recommends thoughtfulness in choosing a staff member who possesses a strong ability for establishing relationships. The check-ins will allow Will to be monitored and to have his backpack and pockets checked, but in a caring manner so that he understands that the process is designed to support, not punish.

Will has no reliable adult connections at this point, so the team determines that it is a priority to build additional adult relationships through mentoring. In addition to the staff member who will be conducting the daily check-ins, the team asks two other alternative education staff members (a math teacher and an instructional assistant) to reach out and welcome Will to the school as well as to build plans to support him academically.

The team reviews Will's protective factors and inhibitors and finds that he is currently lacking but has had prior interest in music and art. Members recommend building those back into Will's life through classes at school, community lessons, or mentorship from music or art teachers. The team discusses the availability of grant funding so the district can possibly pay for lessons, increasing protective factors and prosocial belonging. The lessons will also help him spend his time in a constructive activity, facilitate positive interests, and connect him to the adults and peers involved.

The assessment revealed that Will experiences stress due to his family's financial difficulties. The student threat assessment team has a pool of money (collected through grants and fundraisers) used for building protective factors and decreasing stressors for students, so they discuss offering funding for new clothing and school supplies to assist in building Will's confidence.

The team recommends giving Will an office pass so that when he is stressed or agitated or perceives that he is being harassed, he can seek out the counselor or school administrator to process those feelings and attempt to build resilience and coping strategies. The team also determines that staff members who supervise him will need to know the basic details of Will's situation, since his ideation involved a potential school attack. They will be encouraged to connect with him at school, observe his behavior and communications, and report any concerns to the school administrator.

As an immediate safety precaution, the team asks Will's parents to deliver Will to school in the morning directly to the office for his check-in and pick him up immediately after school. The parents are hesitant at first but agree to the plan because the situation has increased their fear and worry.

School staff members, the law enforcement officer, and the probation officer instruct the parents on safety proofing the house and increasing Will's supervision, which includes monitoring his communications and internet use. The team assists the parents in identifying potential triggers. It also discusses strategies on how to intervene and how Will's parents can recognize when to provide the school with information about concerns or positive developments.

The school team strongly encourages both individual and family counseling, which is supported by the probation officer as well. The team also considers a mentoring program available through the YMCA and brainstorms a number of activities and events that will not only keep Will busy but hopefully connect him with prosocial adults in the community.

The team schedules a date to review the situation, coinciding with Will's release from juvenile detention. Depending upon the situation at that time, the team will add to or adapt the plan. It also schedules routine reviews every two weeks so the administrator can check in with teachers, counselors, and parents to determine whether the interventions are successful and whether Will is improving. When a mental health provider becomes involved, team members will request a release of information from the parents so they can communicate with the provider and include him or her in Will's intervention plan.

Finally, as a restorative measure, the team schedules a meeting with Will and his parents to assess their recognition of the damaging impact of Will's behavior and, at the same time, assess the family's willingness to have a discussion with Daniel and his parents about the impact of the disruptive behavior. If they are willing, the conversation can also address the fear that Will's behavior might have caused, as well as the bullying, and possibly build a bridge to a healthy relationship.

ALISON

Because of significant concerns about targeted violence, the team determines that a referral for a Level 2 assessment is immediately necessary. The following is a discussion of strategies by both the Level 1 and Level 2 teams, with participation by the school team, the district threat assessment lead, a law enforcement officer, and a public mental health specialist. Al's parents were notified but were unwilling to engage in this process.

The team determines that its first priority is to notify the parents or guardians of the potential targets. Because of the serious nature of the threats and the detail that will be provided, the law enforcement officer agrees to collaborate with the school administrator to make the contacts. The team determines that developing plans to protect the students will be crucial to maintaining their safety and will provide them with confidence and peace of mind. The administrator agrees to check in with the students and their parents to confirm that there is no ongoing contact with Al.

Al receives a mental health evaluation because of the peace officer hold. She will likely be released within a day or two, so the team knows it needs to build a plan for her safe return to the community. Al's parents notify the school that she will not be returning to campus; however, in order to improve the physical and psychological safety at the school, the team requests added security in the short term, and the law enforcement officer requests an increase in patrol around the school neighborhood.

The team discusses the specifics of Al's graduation plan and notes that she has only a few classes to complete. Since she will not be returning to her school, she needs an option that provides a pathway to a diploma while also building the trusting relationships she craves, focusing her away from her anger.

The local community college has a seat on the community-based team and has agreed to allow Al to complete her credits through its system, which secures her diploma and provides her with the opportunity to spend time with adult students and instructors whom she might perceive as more mature and intelligent than her current peers (a source of frustration identified by her in her earlier communications).

The community college representative also offers to work with Al on pursuing future university options that meet her needs, which the team sees as a potentially strong motivation. As the representative works with Al, she will explore housing options and coach Al on becoming an adult and making her own choices, which might reduce her stress. She also informs the team that the college has two clubs for members of the LGBTQ community that Al might be interested in joining.

The mental health professional who completed Al's mental health evaluation quickly builds a rapport with her. With that trust and response, Al accepts biweekly therapy sessions with him, along with the management strategies and the academic plan. She also agrees to follow a personal safety plan and immediately communicate any ideation that might lead to harm. In her earlier communications, Al stated that she wanted help from a psychologist she trusted and is now eager and hopeful about her new relationship with someone from the mental health profession. The mental health provider agrees to work with Al until she is stabilized.

Al's sister is also a positive connection in her life, so the team asks the mental health representative if he can assist Al in contacting her sister for support. A potential obstacle the team discusses is that Al's girlfriend's parents have stated that Alex can no longer have contact with Al. This has the potential to be a significant stressor and/or accelerator, so the team asks the mental health representative to monitor Al's perspective on this and assist her with identifying coping skills.

Additionally, the mental health professional shares his plan to engage Al in dialectical behavioral therapy (DBT), which will assist her in building insight, regulating emotions, and creating and maintaining relationships that have depth and trust.

The team recommends that those who are involved with Al continue to monitor her oral, written, and social media communications for indications of any violence planning, preparation, triggers, or grievances.

A review date is set for two days after the meeting to review Al's current status and revise the plan as needed.

Al's parents did not attend the threat assessment meetings, but the district threat assessment lead continued to attempt to make contact. After a few days, the parents were contacted and stated that they believed the mental health representative was trying to help, so they agreed to a short meeting with the mental health provider and the district threat assessment lead. The lead outlined the concerns for targeted violence and the management strategies the team recommended.

Al's parents were somewhat hostile but did agree to remove all weapons from the home and to allow Al to attend the community college. They also agreed to consider allowing her to use campus housing while finishing up her credits. They did not agree to notify anyone if they had ongoing concerns, but they were provided with contact information for those who could assist.

SAM

The team discusses Sam's needs as a student with multiple disabilities and highly reactive, aggressive behavior when confronted with certain triggers. Though Sam was not engaging in targeted aggression, he has caused serious injury to others and there was potential for ongoing injury to others without a strong management plan.

Because of the severity of the situation, the team refers the case for a Level 2 assessment for assistance with management planning. The resulting strategies were provided by both the Level 1 and Level 2 teams, which consisted of the school team, IEP case manager, Sam's mother, the group home manager, the district threat assessment lead, a public mental health representative, and a law enforcement officer.

The team believes that the most important part of a plan for Sam will be the removal of triggers for aggression. Since he appears to react aggressively when working with younger women, the team decides that any staff member working with Sam will be a man or an older woman. If staffing in this manner is a challenge, the teacher will work with the administrator to make sure Sam is not working with someone who is a potential trigger.

In addition, Sam appears triggered by noisy environments, so the team discusses modifications to his schedule to allow him to be in a calm and quiet environment throughout his day. Because this has the potential to alter his IEP service provision, the case manager will also schedule an IEP meeting to discuss these changes and to update Sam's functional behavior assessment with information that was gathered as part of the threat assessment.

The IEP case manager also recommends implementing social stories, designed to teach Sam that his actions do have an impact on others. These social stories will be most effective when read with an adult when Sam's behavior is at baseline. The goal is to highlight empathy and give Sam the opportunity, when at baseline, to acknowledge his own behaviors, which might foster some post-incident debriefings between Sam and those he has frightened or injured.

Because of Sam's tendency to use items as weapons of opportunity, the team discusses the need for safety proofing in Sam's classroom, other areas of the school where he spends time, and his group home. They agree that Sam should not have access to any sharp or particularly heavy items. In addition, the team recommends that all staff members working with Sam have advanced training in de-escalation techniques. A referral is made to the district behavior team, which can work with the school team on both needs.

The law enforcement officer also recommends that Sam's name and address be flagged in the local law enforcement agency's records system so that any officer responding to the home is aware of Sam's disabilities and can respond appropriately without agitating the situation. Both Sam's mother and the group home workers believe this step to be valuable.

Sam's mother states that she needs support in dealing with Sam's behavior, so the team provides a referral to a parent mentorship program in the community.

A review date is scheduled in several weeks so that the team can examine the intervention strategies and the results of the IEP meeting and determine whether progress is being made.

ERIC

Eric's situation is complicated, has many risk factors, and indicates both targeted aggression and the potential for serious or lethal injury. To address all of the safety needs and to support Eric with intervention, the school team decides to refer the case for a Level 2 assessment. The following management strategies are developed by both the Level 1 and Level 2 teams.

The targeted students and their parents or guardians have been notified (as discussed in the case introduction) and have written apology letters to Eric and his mother. The team also decides to develop plans to protect those students and to routinely follow up with the four students to make sure that they are not bullying or harassing Eric and that he is not approaching them. They also recommend that school staff members continue to check in with Eric to inquire about any troubling interactions he might have with these students or anyone else, so they can solve problems or provide the appropriate interventions.

Because the four boys wrote apology letters and appeared to take responsibility for their actions, it seems appropriate, when and if Eric is ready, to coordinate a restorative meeting with the four boys, their parents, Eric, his mother, and a neutral facilitator. Eric's experience involving domestic violence and unresolved bullying did not allow him to adequately express how the actions of others affected him. Having the opportunity to do so with the four boys and their families might be helpful in fostering his sense of self-worth and the realization that many people do show remorse for their actions, unlike his stepfather.

The team discusses Eric's probable expulsion with the staffers at the alternative school. Team members note that the four students who fueled his grievance attend the neighborhood school, as does Susan, who has now been told by her mother that she can no longer have contact with Eric. The team is concerned because Eric's relationship with Susan has boosted his confidence and self-esteem, so the loss of that connection will likely be a significant stressor. He is also apathetic and withdrawn in his current setting.

The team discusses the potential for a voluntary placement at the alternative school, which Eric has already agreed to for at least one week, and identifies a staff member at that school who has an impressive ability to connect with students and who is an excellent male role model—something Eric is lacking. The team recommends that this staff member connect with Eric quickly to attempt to establish that relationship.

When Eric attends school, his belongings will be checked by a staff member, with a supportive attitude and ongoing encouragement for nonaggressive problem solving. In addition, Eric will need an adult mentor or mental health provider to process his separation from Susan and continue to develop coping strategies and skills for nonaggressive problem solving.

The team discusses the potential for one of Eric's mentors to explore his view of power and to identify the pathological thinking that he appears to be unaware of. The team discusses the need for modeling healthy behavior and thinking, which could make a significant difference in the way Eric views his future, his relationships, and his problem-solving decisions.

The team recommends that Eric's communications and mood should be monitored by involved staff members. Attempts to connect Eric with prosocial students to foster relationships are discussed. The team also recommends working with Eric on long-term educational or vocational goals.

Eric is highly interested in Krav Maga, though he has been researching this independently, so the team suggests involvement in a structured martial arts program that will give him access to an adult mentor and instruction in the appropriate use of martial arts.

The team discusses the potential options for approaching Eric's mother and providing her with support, with hopes that she will partner with the district or community providers in Eric's intervention. The team determines that the mentor at the alternative education school would be the most appropriate person to check in with her to continue to encourage counseling and inquire about her support.

A member of the student threat assessment team also has a professional connection with a provider at the local domestic violence victims' support program who is also Asian-American and might be a resource for Eric's mother and assist her in coping with her trauma.

Because of the potential for dating aggression in Eric's situation, a referral is made to a domestic violence intervention program for Eric as well.

Given Susan's potential victimization and the team's concerns about her mother's reaction to the situation, the team decides to have Susan's school counselor routinely check in with her to inquire about potential contact with Eric and to privately discuss the dynamics of healthy relationships.

MAYA

If Maya were subject to a zero-tolerance discipline policy, she would likely be expelled for having the weapons at school, regardless of the context of the possession. In fact, her expulsion would remove most of her protective factors (positive peer exposure, teacher connections, her role in the school musical and band, her academic momentum, etc.) and likely increase her anxiety, depression, disconnection, and sense of loss. Maya, who is functioning well and safely at school, would be at far greater risk if expelled.

Fortunately, she attends school in a district that does not use zero tolerance as a disciplinary policy and that has utilized the preventive threat assessment to examine the event contextually. The Level 1 assessment determines that Maya's situation does not pose a risk of aggression, so there is no need for an ongoing management plan. However, the team identifies a couple of strategies that might benefit Maya. First, it recommends developing an accountability plan that clearly identifies the expectation that Maya will not bring weapons of any kind to school and the potential consequences that would result if she does.

Maya is involved in several positive activities at school and in the community. Team members discuss how Maya and her friends would benefit from an adult mentor who could assist with their interest in fantasy gaming and ensure that their play is appropriate for the school setting. The administrator knows one science teacher who is particularly interested in Dungeons & Dragons and will inquire about that teacher's interest in initiating an after-school club with these students.

The team will also monitor for any new concerns regarding Maya or her passion for collecting knives and swords.

To help confirm that Maya understands the concerns about and impact of bringing weapons to school and to restore any loss of confidence among staff members, the administrator schedules a meeting with Maya, her father, the school counselor, the drama teacher, and a peer of Maya's choosing. The meeting gives Maya the opportunity to hear directly from others about their concerns regarding her choice to bring the weapons to school. Additionally, this meeting gives Maya the opportunity to share her need for a safe place within the school for students with similar interests (Dungeons & Dragons, etc.) to meet and socialize without feeling marginalized.

Beyond this, the team believes there are no other concerns for aggression or needed support that warrant additional intervention.

ALAN

The Level 1 team decides that although there is the concern for potential targeted aggression directed at Alan's grandmother, the situation is manageable by the school team (which includes a law enforcement officer), so it will only consult with the district threat assessment lead about management options rather than refer for a complete Level 2 assessment.

Since the team considers Alan's grandmother to be the primary target, members discuss their duty to warn her. Alan's mother is part of the Level 1 team and offers to have her mother come to the school to meet and discuss the situation. She also states that she will reduce Alan's contact with his grandmother. A creative recommendation is made to enroll Alan in a culinary class so he can learn to cook for himself and his siblings in the evenings, thus relying less on his grandmother's care.

Alan will be provided with a plan that allows him to identify triggers, agitators, and sources of anger, then report to a safe place to process his emotions and receive the appropriate intervention.

The Level 1 team confirms that Alan's father has removed the firearms from his home and coaches him on activities that could replace target shooting.

The team discusses the need to move Alan away from his focus on violence and a zombie apocalypse. Alan has multiple positive relationships with staff members, so the team will encourage those teachers to continue to facilitate relationships with Alan. It will also seek grant money to assist the parents with summer activities such as band camp, music lessons, and other events of interest to Alan, which will keep him focused and busy.

The school will also provide greater access to reading material that is free of violent themes and is prosocial in nature. The school and the parents will carefully monitor Alan's technology use for inappropriate material. The team makes a referral to the district social worker to support Alan's parents in searching for and blocking inappropriate content. It also discusses the potential for the social worker to assist the family in revisiting mental health services for Alan as he processes his feelings about his grandmother.

As a restorative measure, the school counselor offers Alan the opportunity to meet with Carlos. As the Level 1 assessment indicated, Alan and Carlos have had a longstanding conflict. A meeting between the two boys (facilitated by the school counselor) will give both Alan and Carlos the opportunity to share their frustrations and move forward by negotiating an accountability agreement.

The team then circles back to Alan's statement about his friend Chris, who talked about reenacting Columbine the previous year. The assistant principal schedules a time to further investigate the situation and speak with Chris to identify any potential needs or safety concerns.

LEVEL 1 CASE FOLLOW-UP

As noted earlier, at the end of the Level 1 protocol, you will find a section to enter follow-up notes and an ongoing narrative regarding the case. With the exception of Maya, all of the cases reviewed in this book required the development of a management plan that continued to be reviewed by members of the Level 1 team until it was determined that the safety concerns had significantly decreased.

During reviews and updates, the team should note any changes to the student's situation (e.g., an increase or decrease in risk factors, the addition or loss of inhibitors, decreasing or increasing attack-related ideation, progress with the restoration of relationships, progress with intervention, success with counseling or other mental health services, etc.) and make any necessary changes to the management plan.

The team should continue to engage in this reassessment and ongoing management process until there is reason to believe, through a review of risk factors, that the situation no longer poses a concern for targeted or extreme aggression. At this point, the case can be retired.

HOW TO RETIRE A CASE

Threat assessments and prevention work are fluid. Once the risk factors are identified and then addressed through prevention and intervention strategies, success can be identified through informal staffing and conversations with parents, teachers, the student, and other school personnel. As items from the supervision plan are completed or seen as successful, the team should informally reassess the situation and retire the case if the risk of severe injury or targeted violence has been eliminated. The decision is noted, along with the reasons for retiring the case, in the Review Notes at the end of the Level 1 form (see the appendix).

TEST YOURSELF

1. When a target or targets are identified and might be at risk of being harmed, one precautionary step is to:
    a. Send them far, far away.

b. Contact their guardians and provide adequate warning to ensure their safety.
   c. Determine whether they did something wrong that would cause them to be targeted.
2. The following are management strategies that can be used as preventive steps in de-escalating potential violence:
   a. Increase public awareness of the situation through social media.
   b. Pursue expulsion immediately.
   c. Build relationships and connections within the school setting.
   d. Use punitive measures to make an example of the student.
3. When a team is using a restorative conference or meeting as an intervention strategy, it is important to note that:
   a. All parties involved must participate, even if they feel unsafe to do so.
   b. Success can occur only if all parties involved take accountability for their part of the problem and are willing to participate in the meeting.
   c. The goal of the meeting is for all involved to apologize and be friends.

Answers: 1-b; 2-c; 3-b

Conclusion

Daniel, Will, Alison, Sam, Eric, Maya, Alan: Did It Work?

> *Inviting compassion into the bloodstream of an institution's agenda or a scholar's purpose is more than productive, more than civilizing, more than ethical, more than humane; it's humanizing.* —Toni Morrison

The goal of behavioral threat assessment and management is to identify concerns for aggression and to move individuals away from a path that is leading toward targeted violence and reroute them to a more positive, prosocial, and connected path. A strength of this approach is the rapid, observable change in a student's situation that occurs as a result of multiple individuals of varied perspectives coming together to solve problems, share resources, encourage the positive growth of students, and keep them in school.

While each of the seven student situations discussed within this book had a different outcome, engaging the student threat assessment system led to peaceful resolutions as well as access to a variety of interventions and support for these students and their families.

DANIEL

Though Daniel was impulsive, he was generally a compassionate student and was concerned when he heard about Will's perception of him. This reflection, along with the support he received from his parents, his school counselor, and his mental health therapist, led to a desire to increase his coping skills and decrease his impulsive, reactive aggression. Subsequently, he was determined to be eligible for a Section 504 plan, with accommodations to allow access to a staff member when needed and academic accommodations to increase his focus.

On one occasion, after a spoken altercation with a student regarding a TikTok video about a masculine dance jam, Daniel engaged in a brief, mutual physical fight. However, after that incident, Daniel calmed down and sought out his counselor to get support and to discuss his accountability. He was then able to sit down with the other student for a restorative conference, resulting in an agreement that the two boys would not exacerbate the situation by discussing it with their separate friend groups and that they would respectfully keep their distance from each other.

During Daniel's senior year, his counselor worked with him on accessing a career and technical education program in residential construction. Daniel graduated on time with a regular diploma and went on to work as a carpenter part time while attending college to study engineering.

WILL

Since Will was arrested, he was assigned a probation officer who was also a member of the student threat assessment team (STAT). He was eventually placed on probation and was expelled, and then he attended the district's alternative high school program. Will's relationship with his parents continued to be challenging, but his parents reported that they felt supported by Will's probation officer, who was able to provide the accountability and expectations that they didn't believe they could offer.

Mental health treatment was also a mandatory condition of Will's probation. He was diagnosed with depression, started taking antidepressant medication, and began outpatient treatment. Concerns about ongoing attack-related behavior decreased, then stopped, once Will no longer had contact with Daniel and his friends.

After three months of outpatient mental health treatment and Will's subsequent skill development and stabilization, both Will and Daniel were amenable to a restorative conference that included both boys, their parents, and the counselor as the facilitator. The conference offered Will the opportunity to apologize for the fear he had caused and to share his longstanding and deeply rooted grievance with Daniel, allowing Daniel the chance to take accountability and show remorse for his actions, which he was somewhat unaware of.

In the alternative high school program, Will was initially withdrawn and resisted interactions with peers and adults. The administrator in the school continued to attempt to forge a relationship with Will, met with him a couple of times a week, and persuaded him to try an art class at the school. Will's creative ability impressed the teacher, and the two ended up developing a strong relationship.

Will took two more art classes, and the combination of his interest in this activity and the relationship with the teacher seemed to bring him out of his shell. He recut his mullet with added texture and feathering, inspiring a few other students and one teacher to follow suit. He made two friends at the school who were also quiet but generally kind and positive. He attended the alternative school through his senior year and was able to make up several credits but was still behind schedule for an on-time graduation.

However, Will decided that he wanted to finish his credits at his neighborhood school and returned to that school for a final semester. Though he graduated late, his last semester was positive, he had both peer and adult relationships, and he had a strong interest and ability in art. After graduation, Will decided to find a full-time job and continued to receive the support of his probation officer and mental health provider.

ALISON

Al was a student with significant needs but was invested in getting support. She developed a strong relationship with the mental health representative on STAT and attended outpatient therapy regularly. The dialectical behavioral therapy she received helped teach her the skills to improve her distress tolerance, better regulate her emotions, find alternatives to destructive behaviors, and understand the importance of seeing another person's perspective and having empathy, all key components to maintaining relationships. Her admiration for her therapy led her to explore Stoicism and its philosophical roots, which she embraced as her moral compass and spiritual guide.

She enrolled at the local community college and remarked on how much she enjoyed the new setting and "being away from the immature high school drama." She was able to graduate on time and worked with the community college academic counselor on her future college options. With her strong academic record and extraordinarily high SAT scores, she was accepted to an Ivy League college on the East Coast, despite her parents' objections.

However, after her parents saw that she began to stabilize, they relented somewhat and provided her with guarded approval. In her effort to focus on her mental health, she decided to take a year off before college and moved in with her sister, who had returned to a nearby town to provide support to Al. She struggled with her separation from Alex and her perception of being the student who threatened to kill people, but her bolstered relationships and her new philosophical perspective helped her to develop coping skills and a renewed focus on her future.

SAM

Sam's IEP team took the recommendations provided by the threat assessment team and updated his IEP to reflect the identified needs. He ended the school year with several more instances of aggressive behavior but no injuries to others, in either the school or home setting, most likely because of the reduction in triggers and the vigilance in safety proofing.

A male staff member was moved into Sam's classroom to assist with his needs, and the two formed a reasonably close relationship, at first based on their mutual interest in dinosaurs. Eventually, the staff member became a trusted ally of Sam's—one he would often seek out when he was experiencing stress. Sam remained in the group home, and his mother was able to gain a better understanding of his disabilities and of how she could support him in that setting.

ERIC

Before Eric entered the alternative high school, the behavior specialist who was identified as a potential support for Eric contacted him to set up a meeting prior to his enrollment. Eric and the behavior specialist made a fast connection, since Eric saw him as a strong, tough man who was also vulnerable and encouraged others to be emotionally open. Eric raved about this staff member to his mother, who became curious about how he had developed such a strong relationship with Eric.

The combination of Eric's gaining stability and his consistently voiced admiration for the school and the staff members led Eric's mother to leave her home for the first time in two years to attend a parent-teacher conference, where she met the behavior specialist. She quickly realized why Eric enjoyed speaking with him and began seeking his counsel as well. He encouraged Eric's mother to pursue some of the mental health resources recommended by STAT, and with his support, she did. She began meeting with a domestic violence victim's advocate and, much like Eric, began to stabilize and became more open to positive relationships and community supports.

As Eric and his mother slowly began to trust school and community resources and advocates, the behavior specialist mentioned the idea of a restorative conference with the four boys whom Eric identified as his bullies. At first, Eric and his mother were reluctant, but then they decided that the meeting could be what they needed to put the grievance to rest.

The counselor at the alternative school extended the invitations and facilitated the conference. Three of the four boys and their parents accepted the invitation. Eric and his mother were able to express their frustrations to the boys directly, resulting in apologies and a confirmation of the agreements to leave Eric alone.

Even with the support that Eric was receiving, he was not invested in academics and decided to drop out of school during his senior year. However, he remained in contact with the behavior specialist, who encouraged him to consider a GED program. He did so, and after graduation he moved on to the local community college to pursue an automotive mechanics program.

MAYA

Maya was clear that she would never bring knives to school again and did not. She went on to play the lead in *Little Shop of Horrors* and, through some extra tutoring, improved somewhat in trombone. Through this process, she developed a stronger relationship with her school counselor, who met with her a couple of times each month to check in and talk about future options.

The science teacher whom the administrator identified as a possible club lead was not able to take on the task, but a student teacher at the school was interested in the option. She started the Fantasy, Gaming, Science Fiction, and Anime Club (FGSFA) during Maya's senior year, which quickly drew in a large group of students and became Maya's favorite part of her senior year. She graduated from high school with a plan to attend college.

ALAN

Alan's mother followed through on limiting contact between Alan and his grandmother. She still needed help at home, so the school assisted her with a plan to have Alan participate in after-school music activities while his grandmother cared for his siblings in his home. He attended outpatient counseling for several months, after which the therapist assessed that he had gained the coping skills sufficient to address his anger and no longer needed ongoing treatment.

After the threat assessment management strategies were implemented and mental health treatment was reestablished, the school counselor revisited, with Alan, the idea of a restorative conference with Carlos. Both boys agreed and participated in the conference, in which some misunderstandings were discovered and rectified. Both boys apologized for their actions, real or perceived, and agreed that any anger and resentment were over. They remained friendly, and both eventually participated in high school band, without incident.

Alan had no additional instances of threats or aggression at school and continued to have positive interactions with multiple staff members. He went on to high school and became very involved in several music groups and a drama production.

Throughout this book, you have been exposed to the concepts of preventive behavioral threat assessment, identifying risk factors for targeted violence, and the prevention of extreme aggression using a collaborative, multidisciplinary, and user-friendly assessment and management system. It is hoped that these case studies will assist your teams with ideas that are reasonable and fair, that limit the potential impact of bias, and that support students by increasing inclusion and connection as you implement and practice the preventive behavioral threat assessment and management process.

Threat assessment and management is not a panacea for all concerns related to student behavior, but with an established process and trained team members who focus on prevention, inclusion, and the restoration of relationships, schools and communities can move students away from a dangerous pathway toward possible violence or arrest and onto a constructive and supportive trajectory that leads to healthy experiences, education, and employment that foster productive and enjoyable lives.

Appendix
Level 1 Team Assessment Protocolsand Forms

Below is a collection of forms and protocols for the Salem-Keizer Cascade Model. Please visit vandrealconsulting.com and click on Resources/PDF Forms to view and download the following fillable versions.

PREVENTIVE BEHAVIORAL THREAT ASSESSMENT K-12 SCHOOL SITE LEVEL 1 ASSESSMENT FORMS

- Level 1 Protocol 2020 Generic Fillable PDF
- Threat Response Dismissal Form
- 24J Guide
- Plan to Protect Targeted or Victimized Student Fillable PDF
- Notification Log Fillable PDF
- Recommended Notification Letter Fillable PDF
- Level 1 Student Interview
- Level 1 Student Witness Interview Fillable PDF
- Parent Interview Fillable PDF
- Teacher Questionnaire Fillable PDF
- Risk Factors STAT Brochure

PREVENTIVE BEHAVIORAL THREAT ASSESSMENT K-12 COMMUNITY TEAM LEVEL 2 ASSESSMENT FORMS

- Level 2 LEUR Investigation Fillable PDF

- Level 2 Student Interview Fillable PDF
- Level 2 Law Enforcement Fillable PDF
- Level 2 Mental Health Fillable PDF

References and Resources

REFERENCES

Brewster, T., Louallen, S. 2016. "Restorative Justice & the School-to-Prison Pipeline." 4.0 Schools. Accessed July 22, 2021. https://medium.com/future-of-school/restorative-justice-the-school-to-prison-pipeline-5b24280d3d3

Calhoun, F. 1998. *Hunters and Howlers: Threats and Violence Against Federal Judicial Officials in the United States.* Virginia: FBI.

Cornell, D., Maeng, J. 2018. "Racial/Ethnic Parity in Disciplinary Consequences Using Student Threat Assessment." https://nij.ojp.gov/library/publications/racialethnic-parity-disciplinary-consequences-using-student-threat-assessment

Costello, B., Wachtel, J., Wachtel, T. 2019. *The Restorative Practice Handbook: For Teachers, Disciplinarians and Administrators, Second Edition.* Bethlehem, PA: Piper's Press.

Federal Bureau of Investigation. 2015. "Making Prevention a Reality." Quantico, VA. https://www.fbi.gov/file-repository/making-prevention-a-reality.pdf/view

Federal Commission on School Safety. 2018. "The Final Report of Federal Commission on School Safety." https://www2.ed.gov/documents/school-safety/school-safety-report.pdf

Fein, R., Vossekuil, B., and Holden, G. 1995. *Threat Assessment: An Approach to Prevent Targeted Violence.* U.S. Department of Justice.

Fein, R., Vossekuil, B., Pollack, W., Borum, R., Modzeleski, W., Reddy, M. 2002. *Threat Assessment in Schools: A Guide to Managing Threatening Situations and to Creating Safe School Climates.* U.S. Secret Service National Threat Assessment Center, U.S. Department of Education, National Institute of Justice.

Gelles, M., Sasaki-Swindle, K., Palarea, R. 2002. "Threat Assessment: A Partnership Between Law Enforcement and Mental Health." *Journal of Threat Assessment*, Vol. 2 (1) 55–66.

Kirwan Institute for the Study of Race and Ethnicity. 2012. "Understanding Implicit Bias." Ohio State University. https://kirwaninstitute.osu.edu/article/understanding-implicit-bias

Lyubansky, M. 2021. "Nine Criticisms of School Restorative Justice." Accessed February 15, 2021. https://www.psychologytoday.com/us/blog/between-the-lines/201903/nine-criticisms-school-restorative-justice

May, A. 2018. "Ending the School to Prison Pipeline Takes Restorative Justice." The Marcus Harris Foundation. Accessed July 20, 2021. https://marcusharrisfoundation.org/blog/f/ending-the-school-to-school-prison-pipeline-takes-restorative-justice

Meloy, J.R. 2000. *Violence Risk and Threat Assessment: A Practical Guide for Mental Health and Criminal Justice Professionals.* San Diego: Specialized Training Services.

National Association of School Psychologists. 2020. "Behavioral Threat Assessment and Management (BTAM): Best Practice Considerations for K-12 Schools." https://www.nasponline.org/resources-and-publications/resources-and-podcasts/covid-19-resource-center/crisis-and-mental-health-resources/behavioral-threat-assessment-and-management-(btam)best-practice-considerations-for-k%E2%80%9312-schools

Oregon Education Investment Board: Equity Lens. 2014. https://www.oregon.gov/ode/students-and-family/equity/equityinitiatives/Documents/OregonEquityLens.pdf

Salem-Keizer School Board: Equity Lens. 2017. https://mk0salkeizk12or7kyfk.kinstacdn.com/wp-content/uploads/2017/12/Equity-Lens-9-12-2017.pdf

Van Dreal, J., Cunningham, M., Nishioka, V. 2005. "Mid-Valley Student Threat Assessment System: Making Schools Safer Through a Multi-Agency Collaboration." Hamilton Fish Institute. *Persistently Safe Schools*, paper No. 9505, 249–58.

Van Dreal, J., McCarthy, C., Swinehart, R., Okada, D., Rainwater, A., Speckmeier, M., Elliott, S., Rutledge, S., Byrd, R., Novotney, D., Mendoza, D. 2017. *Assessing Student Threats: Implementing the Salem-Keizer System, Second Edition.* Lanham, MD: Rowman & Littlefield.

Watchel, T., O'Connell, T., Watchel, B. 2010. *Restorative Justice Conferencing: Real Justice and The Conference Handbook.* Pipersville, PA: Piper's Press.

Additional Readings and Sources for Level 1 and Level 2 Assessment Protocols

Calhoun, F. 1998. *Hunters and Howlers: Threats and Violence Against Federal Judicial Officials in the United States.* Virginia: FBI.

De Becker, Gavin. 1998. *The Gift of Fear: Survival Signals That Protect Us from Violence.* New York: Little, Brown and Company.

Drysdale, D., Modzeleski, W., and Simons, A. 2010. *Campus Attacks: Targeted violence Affecting Institutions of Higher Education.* Washington, D.C.: U.S. Secret Service, U.S. Department of Homeland Security, Office of Safe and Drug-Free Schools, U.S. Department of Education, and Federal Bureau of Investigation, U.S. Department of Justice.

Federal Bureau of Investigation. 2015. "Making Prevention a Reality." https://www.fbi.gov/file-repository/making-prevention-a-reality.pdf/view

Fein, R., and Vossekuil, B. 1998. *Protective Intelligence & Threat Assessment Investigations.* U.S. Department of Justice.

Fein, R., Vossekuil, B., and Holden, G. 1995. *Threat Assessment: An Approach to Prevent Targeted Violence.* U.S. Department of Justice.

Fein, R., Vossekuil, B., Pollack, W., Borum, R., Modzeleski, W., Reddy, M. 2002. *Threat Assessment in Schools: A Guide to Managing Threatening Situations and to Creating Safe School Climates.* U.S. Secret Service National Threat Assessment Center, U.S. Department of Education, National Institute of Justice.

Johnson, E. 2000. *Advanced Topics in the Assessment of Youth Violence.* Oregon Forensic Institute.

Meloy, J.R. 2000. *Violence Risk and Threat Assessment: A Practical Guide for Mental Health and Criminal Justice Professionals.* San Diego: Specialized Training Services.

Meloy, J.R. 2006. "The Empirical Basis and Forensic Application of Affective and Predatory Violence." *Australian and New Zealand Journal of Psychiatry*, 40, 539–47.

Meloy, J.R., and Hoffman, J. (Editors). 2021. *International Handbook of Threat Assessment (Second Edition).* Oxford University Press.

Meloy, J.R., Hoffman, J., Guldimann, A. 2012. "The Role of Warning Behaviors in Threat Assessment: An Exploration and Suggested Typology." *Behavioral Sciences and the Law*, 30(3), 256–79, May 2012.

Meloy, J.R., Mohandie, K., Knoll, J.L., Hoffmann, J. 2015. "The Concept of Identification in Threat Assessment." *Behavioral Sciences and the Law*, 33(2-3), 213–37, June 2015.

O'Toole, M. 2000. *The School Shooter: A Threat Assessment Perspective.* Federal Bureau of Investigation, Department of Justice.

Pynchon, M.R., and Borum, R. 1999. "Assessing Threats of Targeted Group Violence: Contribution from Social Psychology." *Behavioral Sciences and the Law*, 17:339–55.

Reddy, M., Borum, R., Berlund, J., Vossekuil, B., Fein, R., and Modzeleski, W. 2001. "Evaluating Risk for Targeted Violence in Schools: Comparing Risk Assessment, Threat Assessment, and Other Approaches." John Wiley & Sons, Inc. *Psychology in the Schools*, Vol. 38(2).

United States Secret Service National Threat Assessment Center. 2019. "Protecting America's Schools: A U.S. Secret Service Analysis of Targeted School Violence."

Vossekuil, B., Fein, R., Reddy, M., Borum, R., Modzeleski, W. 2002. "The Final Report and findings of the Safe Schools Initiative: Implications for the Prevention of School Attacks in the United States." U.S. Secret Service National Threat Assessment Center, U.S. Department of Education, National Institute of Justice.

RESOURCES

John Van Dreal Consulting
Salem, OR
vandrealconsulting.com
johnvandreal@gmail.com

J. Reid Meloy, PhD, ABPP
A Forensic Psychological Corporation
Tel. 858-922-1528; Fax 858-551-8096
DrReidMeloy.com
facebook.comDrReidMeloy

Koshka Foundation
Seattle, WA
koshkafoundation.org

Public Consulting Group
https://www.publicconsultinggroup.com/
EDPlan Student Behavioral Threat Assessment and Suicide Risk Assessment Solution
http://www.pcgus.com/bta
Preventive Behavioral Threat Assessment Courses Online
https://www.publicconsultinggroup.com/insights/emerging-solutions/salem-keizer-cascade-bta-courses-by-john-van-dreal/

Robert Martin
Robert Martin Enterprises
Tel. 818-505-0177; 310-344-0570
bob@rmartinenterprises.com

Seth Elliott Consulting
Bend, OR
selliottconsulting.com

Foresight Security Consulting
Portland, OR
foresight-sc.com/about-us

Center for Integrated Intervention
Lake Oswego, OR
integratedintervention.org

Specialized Training Services
P.O. Box 28181
San Diego, CA 92198
1-800-848-1226
info@specializedtraining.com
specializedtraining.com

Gene Deisinger, PhD
Deisinger Consulting, LLC
gdeisinger@deisingerconsulting.com
540-392-5284

Scalora and Associates
scalorassoc@gmail.com

Joseph L. Parks Consulting and Law Office
https://www.josephlparks.com/
972-408-8573

Holifield Psychological Services, Inc.
San Luis Obispo, CA 93405
805-305-4229
drholifield@HPSpsych.org

Manny Tau, PsyD, CTM
888-949-5150
Orange County, CA
www.NoThreat.com

Association of Threat Assessment Professionals
1215 K Street No. 2290
Sacramento, CA 95814
916-231-2146

Crisis Management Institute
cmionline.com
Salem, OR
503-585-3484

Eric M. Johnson, PhD, ABPP
Oregon Forensic Institute
1942 NW Kearney, Suite 21
Portland, OR 97209
503-274-4017

Factor One
P.O. Box 1772
San Leandro, CA 94577
510-352-8660

Gavin de Becker and Associates
11684 Ventura Blvd, Suite 440
Studio City, CA 91604

The Metis Group Inc.
P.O. Box 829
Haymarket, VA 20168
themetisgroupinc.com
571-284-5142

National Center for the Analysis of Violent Crime
FBI Academy
Quantico, VA 22135

The Safe School Initiative
Final Findings
Education Publications Center
U.S. Department of Education
P.O. Box 1398
Jessup, MD 20794
1-877-433-7827

About the Authors

John Van Dreal is a school psychologist and the retired director of Safety and Risk Management Services for the Salem-Keizer School District. He continues his career consulting with school districts and communities on behavioral threat assessment systems and operational security. He has over 35 years of experience in threat assessment and management, psychoeducational evaluation, crisis intervention, behavioral intervention, and security and risk management systems consultation.

In 1999, he began the development and implementation of the Salem-Keizer Cascade Model, a multiagency student threat assessment system considered by experts to be a leading practice. Through that collaboration, he has worked daily with educators, law enforcement, trial court personnel, juvenile justice, and mental health personnel in preventive behavioral threat assessment—the management of youth and adult threats of aggression within the schools, institutions, and the community. He served as chair of Oregon's Mid-Valley Student Threat Assessment Team from its inception in 2000 through 2015 and continues to provide consultation to its membership. He has served as a member of the Marion County Threat Advisory Team since 1999.

He is the editor and principal author of the book *Assessing Student Threats: Implementing The Salem-Keizer System, Second Edition*. He has advised on, or contributed to, a number of threat assessment guides, including the *International Handbook of Threat Assessment, Second Edition*; *Threat Assessment in the Schools: A Guide to Managing Threatening Situations and to Creating Safe School Climates* (United States Secret Service and United States Department of Education); and *Making Prevention a Reality: Identifying, Assessing, and Managing the Threat of Targeted Attacks* (Behavioral Analysis Unit, National Center for the Analysis of Violent Crime). He has been interviewed by a number of television, radio, and print news outlets, including National Public Radio, Oregon Public Broadcasting, Mother Jones, Esquire, and HBO.

John regularly provides training and consultation to audiences nationally on threat assessment systems, preventing and mitigating human violence, school security, and response options for violent intruder and active shooter situations.

He is dedicated to his own community, patronizing locally owned establishments and supporting nonprofit arts and human services organizations. He is a musician, a published poet, and a nationally renowned fine artist with paintings in several notable collections. Finally, he is lucky to be the partner of a gifted school counselor, and he is a proud father of two brilliant adult children and a loving companion to two pets.

About the Authors

Courtenay McCarthy is the lead school psychologist in student preventive behavioral threat assessment and management for Salem-Keizer Public Schools, is chair of the Mid-Valley Student Threat Assessment Team, and is a member of the Marion County Threat Advisory Team. While partnering with John Van Dreal, she has refined the Salem-Keizer student threat assessment system to reflect leading practice in behavioral threat assessment, violence prevention, early intervention, and equitable practices.

Courtenay has over two decades of experience in prevention, threat assessment and management, psychoeducational evaluation, intervention with at-risk youth and families, and behavioral consultation and intervention. As a certified threat manager and nationally certified school psychologist, she regularly provides training and consultation on student threat assessment systems implementation and youth violence to school districts and community agencies throughout the nation. She also provides workshops, symposiums, and content presentations to national audiences. In addition, Courtenay is a contributing author to the book *Assessing Student Threats: Implementing the Salem-Keizer System—Second Edition* (Van Dreal et al., 2017).

When she's away from the office, Courtenay spends time finding adventures, both local and distant, with her husband, John, and daughter, Teagan.

Coleen Van Dreal is a school counselor at Roberts High School @ Chemeketa, Salem-Keizer Public School's alternative high school. She serves as an advocate, academic and vocational counselor, and mental health support for at-risk, marginalized students who have not found success or necessary personalized resources in traditional, comprehensive high school settings. With over two decades of experience in the field of mental health and school counseling, she coaches and guides her students as they work toward credit recovery, graduation, and the development of a successful post–high school education or vocational plan.

As a mental health crisis responder, Coleen was a member of the Mid-Valley Student Threat Assessment Team from 2001 to 2002. She currently serves as a representative for alternative education on the Marion County Threat Advisory Team. Most recently, Coleen has become an advocate for the implementation of restorative practices within the schools.

When she's not working, Coleen enjoys spending time with her family, reading a good book, drinking bubbles and wine, and enjoying happy hour with her husband, John.

www.ingramcontent.com/pod-product-compliance
Lightning Source LLC
Chambersburg PA
CBHW020125240426
43673CB00038B/593